BEST PRACTICES FOR YOGA WITH VETERANS

YOGA SERVICE BEST PRACTICES GUIDE: VOLUME TWO

BEST PRACTICES FOR YOGA WITH VETERANS

Presented by the Yoga Service Council and the Omega Institute

EDITOR

Carol Horton, Ph.D.

CONTRIBUTING EDITORS

Susan Pease Banitt, LCSW, RYT, Lilly Bechtel, Lisa Danylchuk, LMFT, E-RYT, P.K. Lillis, MD, MHA, COL(ret), Michael Huggins, MBA, E-RYT, P. S. Eggleston, MS, MBA, E-RYT

CONTRIBUTORS

A. Arbogast, LICSW, RYT
Peter Banitt, MD
Beryl Bender Birch, E-RYT
Y. Calhoun, MA, MS, E-RYT
Jessica Coulter, MA, RYT
James Fox, MA
Ben King, MA, CPT, RYT
O. Kvitne, E-RYT, YACEP
Marianne Leas
Suzanne Manafort
D. Turner, MBA, RYT, Maj. USAF
Annie Okerlin, E-RYT
S. Plummer Taylor, MSW, RYT
Ann Stevens, CYI, ERYT
Charlene Sams, RYT
A. Schoomaker, RN, E-RYT
Kathryn M. Thomas, E-RYT
Ned Timbel, RYT
Judy Weaver, E-RYT
Alison Whitehead, MPH, RYT

REVIEWERS

Robin Carnes, MBA, E-RYT 500
Janet M. Durfee RN/MSN/ANP-c
Rolf Gates
Kate Hendricks Thomas, Ph.D., E-RYT 200

Note to Readers

The recommendations for teaching and practicing yoga made in Best Practices for Yoga with Veterans are not meant to substitute for the guidance of a qualified physician or mental health provider. Yoga teachers and students alike are encouraged to seek professional expertise as needed to ensure that yoga practices are tailored to fit the health needs of each individual.

All of the findings and conclusions reported in this book are those of the Editor, Contributing Editors, and Contributors, who are solely responsible for its contents. They do not necessarily represent the views of the Department of Veterans Affairs, or the United States Government. No statement in this document should be construed as an official position of the Department of Veterans Affairs.

This book is meant to serve as a supplement to relevant yoga teacher trainings and professional education programs, licensures, or accreditations. It cannot, however, serve as a substitute for them.

YSC-Omega Publications
PO Box 8238. Atlanta GA 31106-0238
Contact: board@yogaservicecouncil.org

ISBN-10: 1539917347
ISBN-13: 978-1539917342

Suggested Citation: Horton, Carol (Ed). (2016). *Best Practices for Yoga With Veterans*. Yoga Service Best Practices Guide Vol 2. Atlanta GA: YSC-Omega Publications.

Cover Photo Credit: Liana Redshaw, special thank you to Kathryn Thomas and Dan Nevins

CONTENTS

WELCOME TO THE SECOND YOGA SERVICE BEST PRACTICES BOOK

The commitment of yoga teachers, doctors, therapists, and others to share yoga, mindfulness, and meditation with veterans—often with powerful results—is deep and impressive. I know many such teachers and healers, and would love to write a book about each of these worthy people. Instead, over the past four years, I've interviewed many of them for my *Huffington Post* series entitled "Yoga, How We Serve." In their interviews, these women and men shared the unique needs of veterans and their families, lessons learned in doing this work, and how existing resources and treatments often do not adequately address this population's needs.

Here is just one of many extraordinary testimonials to the healing power of yoga from a Vietnam War veteran participating in a program called Mindful Yoga Therapy:

> *As I started to practice daily, I noticed several things happening. First, I began to sleep better. Next, I was getting to know myself, for the first time ever. Slowly, I came off all of my psych meds. That was big! For the first time in over 40 years, I was medication-free. Over the years, I've been on over 23 different kinds of medications, from Ativan to Xanax! Yoga is now my therapy.*

This veteran went on to say that he hopes that yoga will someday be offered to all veterans, as well as to all troops during basic training—a hope that I share!

Many of the people I interviewed are national, and even international leaders in the growing field of yoga for veterans. To a substantial extent, the conversations I had with them laid the groundwork for this book. Thanks to the contacts and knowledge gained through my interview series, I was able to work with the Yoga

Service Council (YSC) Board and Omega Institute leadership to start planning what eventually grew into a 25-person working meeting on Yoga with Veterans, held in Fall 2015 at Omega. All of the Contributors to this book attended; together, they co-created the basis for this book.

Best Practices for Yoga with Veterans is the second volume in the YSC's annual Best Practices series. The larger Best Practices Project of which these books are a part began with a conversation among YSC leaders concerning how we might help make the field of yoga service more professional and ethical, effective and sustainable, safe and socially just. We asked ourselves: What events could we convene, what materials could we produce, what could we do in the world that would be truly useful?

With the generous support of the Omega Institute, we decided to invite a group of 25 yoga service leaders dedicated to serving a distinct population, and working in a common organizational context, to participate in a 5-day Best Practices Symposium at Omega each year. The purpose of these Symposia is to facilitate a collaborative process dedicated to building strong relationships in the field, identifying shared Best Practices for teaching yoga to a given constituency, and laying the groundwork for an edited volume elaborating them each year. The culmination of the first round of this process, *Best Practices for Yoga in Schools,* was published in 2015. Now, we are proud to offer *Best Practices for Yoga with Veterans.*

Contributors to this book include yoga teachers, studio owners, doctors, nurses, therapists, journalists, authors, scholars, veterans, veteran family members, VA administrators, and nonprofit leaders. They teach yoga, train yoga teachers, administer integrative health programs, and otherwise support the work of bringing yoga, mindfulness, and meditation practices to veterans in VA facilities, veterans' centers, VFWs, yoga studios, community centers, and other locations nationwide. Most had never met or worked together prior to being invited to the Yoga with Veterans Symposium. All volunteered a week of their time to participate, traveling to the Omega Institute in upstate New York from all over the country to attend.

To co-create this book, everyone involved had to embrace the often difficult work of setting aside their natural attachment to their own particular programs and practices in order to find common ground on what works best for the field. This pooling of diverse sources of knowledge and expertise was necessary to identify the "best" best practices for the wide range of issues facing younger veterans in the wake of America's decade-long wars in Iraq and Afghanistan, as well as aging veterans who served in previous conflicts. These issues include clinical conditions such as post-traumatic stress, depression, and brain injury, as well as social concerns such as family reunification post-deployment and re-integration into civilian life.

Attempting to face such challenges without sufficient medical, therapeutic, and social support all too often produces secondary problems such as addiction, unemployment, domestic abuse, homelessness, and suicide. Tragically, research indicates that such issues plague the veteran population disproportionately. Although therapies and supports do exist to help veterans overcome such challenges, they are often under-resourced and/or under-utilized. My passionate belief, which is shared by the Contributors to this book and supported by a growing body of research, is that yoga, mindfulness, and meditation practices have an important role to play in improving veterans' health, and renewing their overall sense of well-being.

In the end, the Contributors produced the volume in front of you with considerable help from the wonderful writing ability of Editor Carol Horton, guidance of four expert reviewers, and extensive project coordination by Kathryn Monti Thomas. Along with the YSC Board, we are deeply grateful to the Omega Institute for their support of this book, as well as the larger Best Practices Project of which it is a part.

Thank you, all, for bringing these best practices to life.

Yours in service,

Rob Schware
President Ex-Officio and Advisor, Yoga Service Council
Co-Founder, Give Back Yoga Foundation

A MESSAGE FROM THE OMEGA INSTITUTE

Since our beginning, Omega's mission has been to awaken the best in the human spirit and to provide hope and healing for individuals and society. Yoga and service have always been core components of our offering, and continue to serve as transformative tools toward our personal and collective growth and well-being.

Over the years, an ever-widening network of people and organizations that share our deep commitment to service has enriched our community. Through this experience, we have learned that the power of working together is much stronger than walking the path alone. When we combine our energy and intentions, we extend our reach and have a greater positive impact in the world. That's why it's only natural the Yoga Service Council (YSC) and Omega have partnered together on a path to offer and support yoga service.

This partnership began in 2009, when Omega offered space for a group of yoga teachers to come together and talk about ways to support those who worked with vulnerable and underserved populations. The YSC emerged from this initial gathering, and offered the first annual Yoga Service Conference at Omega in 2011.

During each Yoga Service Conference at Omega, we have discovered and rediscovered that the YSC board and others who choose to be involved in this work are some of most compassionate people we have met. Yoga service truly is a practice of the heart—and, a specific path of yoga that fully aligns with Omega's mission and ideals.

As a result of our shared commitment to yoga and service, the YSC and Omega decided to formally partner in 2014 to bring yoga into the lives of more individuals and communities who have limited access to these vital teachings. We are excited to continue this partnership with the YSC and all its member organizations.

One example of our partnership is the Yoga Service Best Practices guide you are now reading. This project began in 2015, when 30 leaders in the fields of yoga service and veterans affairs came together at Omega to lay the groundwork for the second book in this series, *Best Practices for Yoga with Veterans.* Helping veterans and their families heal from post-traumatic stress through trainings and retreats focused on complementary and alternative healing modalities has been an area of focus at Omega for more than 20 years, and we're pleased to have helped in the development of this vital new guide. We also look forward to the publication of *Best Practices for Yoga for Incarcerated and Court-Involved People* in 2017.

We offer a special thanks to the Yoga with Veterans project team—Rob Schware, Kathryn Monti Thomas, Carol Horton, and Charlene Sams—as well as the entire YSC board for their important work in the world. We're honored to be your partners on this journey.

With deep appreciation,

Robert "Skip" Backus
Chief Executive Officer
Omega Institute

EDITOR'S INTRODUCTION

Not long ago, "yoga for veterans" may have sounded odd to many ears. Today, yoga's popularity among veterans, as well as military personnel more generally, is growing fast. And with good reason: When adapted to meet the needs, concerns, and values of service members and their families, yoga is an exceptional resource for building health, strength, and resilience, both physically, psychologically, and emotionally.

Best Practices for Yoga with Veterans is a vital resource for anyone interested in accessing, delivering, or learning about high-quality yoga programming for veterans. The product of an innovative collaborative process, this book encapsulates the collective knowledge, insights, and experience of over 30 people, and a year-and-a-half's worth of work.

Together, the Contributors, Editors, and Reviewers who co-created this book have expertise not only in yoga, mindfulness, and meditation, but also veterans affairs, military operations and culture, medical specialties including cardiology and oncology, nursing, integrative medicine, clinical psychology, social work, trauma therapy, academia, social research, journalism, nonprofit management, and more. Eight are veterans. Many have extensive experience working in Veterans Health Administration Medical Centers (a.k.a., "the VA") as doctors, nurses, therapists and/or yoga instructors. All are passionate about sharing top-quality yoga instruction with veterans because we believe it is a powerful resource for healing, empowerment, and positive change.

Best Practices for Yoga with Veterans integrates experience- and research-based knowledge to produce over 100 Best Practice guidelines for teaching yoga to veterans in ways that are safe, effective, sustainable, and responsive to the particularities of the military experience. These Best Practices are divided into nine user-friendly thematic sections, which include 1) Culture and Communications, 2) Staffing and Training, 3) Working with Trauma, 4) Curriculum and Instruction, 5) Gender Considerations, 6) Relationship Building, 7) Working in the VA, 8) Teaching Incarcerated Veterans, and 9) Teaching Families of Veterans. Collectively, these Best Practices support teaching yoga with veterans in ways that are resonant with military culture, medically sound, trauma-informed, therapeutically appropriate, gender-responsive, personally empowering, socially equitable, and supportive of positive personal and professional relationships.

As used in this book and the Best Practices series of which it's a part, the term "yoga" refers to a set of practices that include postures and movement, breath work, focused attention, and deep relaxation. While the YSC recognizes that the yoga tradition has other critical dimensions, such as philosophical and ethical study, they are outside the purview of this work. We hope all the titles in this series effectively communicate the fact that if yoga is taught and experienced as a holistic mind-body integration practice, it offers inestimably more than its popular image as a stretching-focused fitness modality could ever suggest.

Best Practices for Yoga with Veterans explains why yoga can be such a valuable resource, and what is required to teach it in ways that will enable all veterans, regardless of age, gender, physical ability, or health status, to experience it as a means of supporting healing, resilience, and well-being on both the physical, psychological, and emotional levels. While intended to be engaging to anyone interested in the subject, it was written with three primary audiences in mind. These include:

1) Veterans, veteran family members, and other service members interested in learning more about yoga;

2) Yoga teachers, studio owners, and yoga service providers seeking to serve this population; and

3) VA administrators, veterans' organizations, and others interested in developing yoga programs for veterans, as well as other military personnel.

Given the diversity of these intended audiences, different sections of the book will speak more directly to some than to others. For example, yoga teachers who are unfamiliar with the military might benefit from studying the "Culture and Communications" section carefully. In contrast, veterans and others familiar with the military could simply skim through this section quickly. In general, readers should feel free to skip around through the book, focusing on sections that speak most directly to their interests, concerns, and needs.

Although the sections build on each other logically, it is not necessary to read this book chronologically, from start to finish. Each section should be comprehensible on its own terms. Additionally, many parts cross-reference others, directing readers to other sections particularly relevant to a given discussion. That said, *Best Practices for Yoga with Veterans* offers such a wealth of information that all readers should find it engaging, educational, and valuable, regardless of personal experience and work-related expertise.

Although this book focuses on the U.S., the principles and practices it presents should transfer fairly easily to other contexts. For example, the human experience of trauma is transcultural, as are many, if not most of the yoga techniques that can help heal it. Similarly, although the specifics of organizational structure and military culture discussed in this work would obviously need to be changed in order to apply the Best Practices presented to a different national context, the core principles they represent should in most cases be able to stand unchanged.

It's important to acknowledge that this book, as well as the Best Practices series of which it's a part, could not have been produced without the generous support of the Omega Institute. We at the Yoga Service Council are deeply grateful for our ongoing partnership with Omega, which enables us to pursue our passion for yoga service in ways we could never replicate otherwise. Personally, I'd also like to thank my fellow members of the YSC Board of Directors—Jennifer Cohen Harper (President), Bob Altman (Treasurer), Charlene Sams (Secretary),

Kathryn Monti Thomas (Project Manager), Susanna Barkataki, Brett Cobb, and Mark Lilly—whose hard work, enthusiasm, and commitment to yoga service are a continual source of inspiration. Special thanks are similarly due to Rob Schware and Traci Childress, who also played a pivotal role in getting the Best Practices series off the ground.

In closing, I'd like to once again thank the 25 Contributors to *Best Practices for Yoga with Veterans,* six of whom also served as Contributing Editors, drafting core segments of the text. A truly wonderful group of human beings, they made this book possible by generously sharing their time, experience, and expertise. Equal thanks are due to our four expert reviewers, who donated the time necessary to read the working manuscript closely, helping to make the final product even better.

All these people committed their hearts and minds to the mission of sharing yoga with veterans, and poured their energy into making it an ever-growing reality. Together, we salute and honor others who share this vision, and are working to bring it to fruition—and extend our thanks and gratitude to you, as well.

Warmly,

Carol Horton, Ph.D.
Vice-President, Yoga Service Council

CULTURE AND COMMUNICATION BEST PRACTICES

Different social groups, institutions, and organizations tend to generate distinct cultural patterns that include approved and disapproved ways of communicating. The military is no exception to this general rule. On the contrary, "warrior culture" is typically a powerful force in the lives of active duty military personnel and veterans alike. Given the intensity of the work they have prepared for and experienced, this is not surprising. As Malmin (2013) explains, "warrior type occupational groups, such as military armed forces personnel, civilian firefighters, law enforcement officers, and other emergency first responders, all work under high levels of stress and often witness inhumanity." These and other shared experiences, including socialization into a shared set of norms and values, generate an "idiosyncratic occupational culture" distinct from that of the majority, civilian population.

As Halvorson (2010) notes, "military culture is ingrained in military personnel from the start of their careers." Each branch of the service is trained to understand and embody its own history, customs, and courtesies, as well as general military ethics and values. Soldiers, Sailors, Airmen, Marines, Coast Guardsmen, Reservists, and National Guardsmen learn to follow behavioral norms such as how to properly wear their uniforms, listen to and follow orders, and function within the military chain of command. Both in initial training and throughout their service, there is a consistent emphasis on personal discipline, mission focus, and emotional control.

While this socialization creates strong bonds among service men and women, the flip side of this cohesion is a tendency to be "exclusive and mistrustful of outsiders with different life experiences" (Hendricks Thomas 2015, 53). In the U.S., this division between warrior and civilian culture has deepened during more than four decades of an all-volunteer force that only involves a small percentage of Americans. The majority of Americans lack a basic understanding of military organization, culture, and terminology, including the vast majority of yoga teachers who are not members of the military or veterans themselves. This missing cultural knowledge is critical to remedy, as something as simple as misusing a key military colloquialism can create an unnecessary barrier between teacher and student.

Consequently, civilian teachers should receive specialized training in military culture and communications before beginning to teach yoga to veterans. Presumably, yoga teachers who are veterans themselves will not need such training. Anyone who has completed a standard yoga teacher training (YTT) program not specially designed to serve military personnel, however, will need to consider how to translate the civilian language and cultural norms it inculcated into parallel practices suitable for veterans. Teaching yoga to veterans requires not only an understanding of such habits, norms, and values, but also an ability to work with them in ways that support the yogic "mission" of increasing health, resilience, and well-being.[1]

CULTURE AND COMMUNICATION 1: LEARN BASICS OF MILITARY ORGANIZATION

Yoga teachers who are unfamiliar with the military should learn the basic structure and accompanying terminology sufficiently to facilitate effective communication with veterans.

Governing Structure. The U.S. Constitution places the military under civilian control. Ultimate authority is vested in the President, who serves as

1 For a set of helpful web-based resources, see VA (2016).

Commander-in-Chief. The U.S. Congress has the power to declare war. The Secretary of Defense serves in the President's Cabinet as chief military advisor. Under the direction of the President, the Secretary directs the Department of Defense (DOD), and serves as second-in-command of the Armed Forces.[2]

The Department of Veterans Affairs (VA) is separate from the DOD. For information on the structure of the VA and how to work with it as a yoga teacher, see the "Best Practices for the VA" section.

Services and Reserves. The U.S. military has five different services: the Army, Air Force, Navy, Marine Corps, and Coast Guard. Each of these branches also has a Reserve, whose members serve in a part-time capacity unless mobilized to serve full time.

The National Guard is a second reserve component. Its members serve part-time unless otherwise activated or deployed. Each state, territory, and the District of Columbia has its own National Guard.

Yoga teachers should understand that some military personnel are sensitive about being confused with members of other services. For example, contrary to what some civilians may assume, not everyone in the military is a "soldier." When working with veterans, learning and using the following titles correctly is critical to build trust:

- The Army has Soldiers
- The Air Force has Airmen
- The Navy has Sailors
- The Marine Corps has Marines
- The Coast Guard has Coast Guardsmen

---

2 As is generally the case in American government today, the actual structure of organization and decision-making is much more complex. For a good discussion of current issues and challenges, see Fallows (2015).

- The Reserve Components have Reservists
- The National Guard has Guardsmen

Military Ranks and Functions. Yoga teachers should similarly understand the structure of different military ranks and functions, and know the terminology associated with them. Most centrally, these include commissioned officers, warrant officers, and enlisted personnel:

- *Commissioned officers* must have a four-year college degree, and predominantly perform management and leadership functions. They also include military personnel who are members of the legal and medical professions, including lawyers, doctors, nurses, and physician assistants. Some helicopter pilots are also officers. Commissioned officers outrank warrant officers and enlisted personnel.
- *Warrant officers* often have college degrees, and perform highly specialized functions (e.g., specialized logistics and certain helicopter pilots).
- *Enlisted personnel* must have either a high school diploma or GED, and perform technical or specialized jobs. Many have some college experience, and may go on to complete a four-year degree, especially as they rise in the ranks. For the most senior ranks, a four-year degree is almost a requirement; many have a MA. Enlisted personal also acquire additional professional skills through military training. Over 75 percent of the military is comprised of enlisted personnel.

Working Status. Yoga teachers should likewise understand different categories of working status among military personnel, including being on active duty versus in the Reserves, and performing combat versus non-combat roles.

Active Duty vs. Reserve: Members of the military who are on active duty serve in one of the five branches, work for the military full time, and can be deployed at any time. They often live on or near military posts or bases with their families and are highly mobile, moving at least once every two to three years. Some, however, will remain posted in a single location for many years, particularly if working with a very unusual skill set. Others living in certain urban areas may switch jobs every few years, but not change their geographic home.

While members of the military who are in the Reserve or National Guard sign on to serve one weekend a month and two full weeks a year, they may be deployed at any time. Since the advent of the Afghanistan conflict in 2001 (OEF) and Iraq War in 2003 (OIF), these personnel have been deployed at a rate and in numbers not seen since World War II.

Combat vs. Non-Combat: Although all military members must be ready to deploy, they will not necessarily have experienced combat. While a large number of military jobs are directly related to combat, many other functions have a supporting role, such as personnel affairs, science, and procurement. The commonly held idea that every person serving in the military is directly involved in combat is inaccurate.

Likewise, not every wounded veteran has been wounded in combat. Yoga teachers should keep in mind that wounded members could be recovering from a variety of diseases, accidents, or other issues that are not combat related.

Veteran Status. Similarly, it is important for yoga teachers to understand both the legal definition and vernacular meaning of term, "veteran."

Under U.S. law, a "veteran" is defined as "a person who served in the active military, naval, or air service, and who was discharged or released therefrom under conditions other than dishonorable." Yoga teachers should be aware, however, that it is not unusual for active military members, Reservists, and Guardsmen to self-identify with the term "veteran" in everyday military culture. For example, a service member might say, "I am a Veteran of Enduring Freedom."

Legally, holding the status of "veteran" is important both for the honor it bestows, and for the rights to VA benefits it confers. Under existing law, the question of whether Reservists and Guardsmen are considered veterans who qualify for VA benefits is somewhat complex. Those who were never called to federal active duty military service do not qualify for VA benefits, unlike those who were activated and served the full period for which they were called. National Guard and Reserve members are also eligible for VA benefits if they were disabled or died from a disease or injury incurred or aggravated in the line of duty, and in selected individual circumstances (Szymendera 2015, 5).

Many of the estimated 100,000 gay service members who were given less-than-honorable discharges between World War II and the 2011 repeal of the "Don't Ask, Don't Tell" (DADT) policy do not qualify as veterans who may receive VA benefits because of the nature of their discharge. Although many are actively working to amend their status, the key legislation that would do so (the "Restore Honor to Service Members Act") has been stalled in Congress since 2013 (Phillips 2015).

Yoga teachers should be sensitive to the fact that such legal issues may be challenging to some of their students. Suggested best practices include following the lead of the military members they are working with in their use of the term "veteran," while striving to be as maximally inclusive and respectful as possible.

CULTURE AND COMMUNICATION 2: LEARN BASICS OF MILITARY CULTURE

Civilians unfamiliar with military culture should familiarize themselves with it by taking specialized trainings, reading relevant materials, and listening to veterans.

Military Values. Each branch of the service has a distinctive organizational culture that includes a set of core values. These values are expected to guide how all service members live their life, as well as how decisions are made and operations executed within the military as a whole. Listed by service, these core values include:

- *Army:* loyalty, duty, respect, selfless service, honor, integrity, and personal courage
- *Navy and Marines:* honor, courage, and commitment
- *Air Force:* integrity, service before self, excellence in all we do
- *Coast Guard:* honor, respect, and devotion to duty

All members of the military are additionally trained to share the core value of "leave no one behind." This means that no fellow service member will ever be left on the field of battle, whether alive or dead. Military personnel are expected to do everything in their power to support each other, even in highly dangerous situations (Halvorson, 9).

Common Stressors and Job Satisfaction. Members of the military services are on duty 24/7, which sometimes means working long hours, weekends and holidays. Common stressors include frequent deployments and military moves, family separation, demands for high physical standards, continuous academic and professional training, challenges in balancing personal life with imposed job demands, not having the ability to resign, and having limited input on new positions and responsibilities.

Members of the Reserves and National Guard face similar stressors due to the high frequency of multiple deployments in the post-9/11 era. Often, these are compounded by a sense of isolation produced by living in civilian communities, separated from fellow members of the military who share common experiences and understandings in ways civilians do not.

Despite such stressors, many aspects of military culture are commonly experienced as personally satisfying. These include a high degree of camaraderie; a shared sense of patriotism; job security and benefits (education, medical, paid leave, travel); professional development and timely promotions; a sense of clarity, transparency, and direction based on rank structure; and sense of service to others, purpose, and duty.

Military Terminology. Similar to other professions, the military has a unique way of communicating. Specialized military language includes acronyms (e.g., CO = Commanding Officer), phrases ("boots on the ground), honorifics ("sir," "ma'am"), and slang ("Wilco"). Yoga teachers unfamiliar with such language should listen carefully to their students, as well as other veterans and military members, and seek to learn and utilize key terms properly. For a partial list of terms and acronyms that may be particularly useful to yoga teachers working with veterans, see the Glossary / Useful Terms listing in the Appendix.

STAFFING AND TRAINING BEST PRACTICES

The study of yoga has traditionally been highly decentralized. Different teachers teach different methods, which vary tremendously in terms of physical challenge, therapeutic benefit, and more. At the same time, yoga remains essentially unregulated in the U.S. Although a few states have sought to license, tax, or otherwise regulate yoga teacher training programs, such efforts have been strongly countered by yoga activists, and generally unsuccessful (Ehrenfreund, 2015).

Although there is no easy way to assess the significance of the most commonly cited yoga teaching credentials, there are important criteria to consider. This section presents recommendations designed to support military professionals and veterans organizations interested in hiring yoga instructors, as well as yoga-based organizations interested in developing their capacity to teach veterans and other military personnel.

STAFFING AND TRAINING 1: UNDERSTAND TEACHING CREDENTIALS

Understand the significance of the most commonly cited teaching credentials in the field.

Although there are no regulations or credentialing requirements governing the teaching of yoga, there is a widely shared, informal norm that instructors should, at a minimum, have completed a 200-hour yoga teacher training (YTT) with a Yoga Alliance (YA) certified program before beginning to teach. Because YA-created credentials are the most common in the field, it is important for military professionals making hiring decisions to have a basic understanding of their significance.

The **RYT Credential.** Yoga Alliance is a nonprofit organization formed in 1999, and the leading professional organization in the field. It is best known for maintaining a voluntary registry of YTT programs that meet its curriculum standards. These standards set the norm of a 200-hour yoga teacher training. In so doing, they specify the number of study hours required for core elements of the training (e.g., teaching methods, anatomy and physiology, principles and ethics). Graduates of teacher training programs registered with YA are authorized to use the widely recognized credential of "RYT 200."[3]

Within the yoga world, it is widely recognized that the YTT programs that confer the RYT credential can and do vary tremendously. Yoga Alliance curriculum guidelines are very general, and different programs interpret and implement them in different ways. In many respects, the resultant diversity is a good thing. Having a variety of yoga methods and philosophies available allows the practice to work equally well for people with varying physical abilities, cultural backgrounds, and so on.

The fact that Yoga Alliance has no means of evaluating the actual operations of the programs it registers is problematic. If YA approves a written curriculum and the organization housing the YTT pays their fee, it becomes a registered program. There is, in other words, no quality control mechanism other than the written application itself. Consequently, it is not surprising that both the content and quality of YTT programs conferring the RYT credential varies enormously.

IAYT and Other Credentials. Although the RYT credentials conferred by Yoga Alliance are the most commonly used in the field, other certifications are available. Most notably, the International Association of Yoga Therapists (IAYT), a national nonprofit organization dedicated to establishing yoga as a "recognized

---

3 There are several additional levels of the RYT credential; for a full list, see Yoga Alliance (2016).

and respected" form of physical and/or psychological therapy, will launch a certification program offering the "C-IAYT" in June 2016.

An increasing number of yoga service organizations (generally, but not exclusively non-profits) also offer specialized training in teaching yoga to veterans and/or trauma-informed yoga. High-quality trainings from reputable organizations of this sort are indispensible to the mission of teaching yoga to veterans effectively, as their offerings are tailored to support it in ways that most yoga trainings are not. To find a high-quality training, it is crucial to invest time in online research and talk directly with knowledgeable people in the field.

STAFFING AND TRAINING 2: MATCH TEACHING CREDENTIALS TO STUDENT NEEDS

Teachers in clinical settings should be required to meet higher minimum standards of training and experience than those working with pre-deployment personnel or in community settings.

Teachers leading classes comprised of physically fit students in pre-deployment settings such as boot camp do not need to be as highly trained and experienced as those working with veterans in the V.A. and other clinical settings. Recommended credentials for pre-deployment settings include:

- RYT 200 status (i.e., at least 200 hours of yoga teacher training with a Yoga Alliance credentialed program, or the equivalent);
- Training in military culture and communications, if needed; and
- Training in trauma-informed yoga.

Training in military culture and communications for yoga teachers is offered by a growing number of yoga service organizations, and indispensible for civilian teachers. "Trauma-informed yoga" is a growing subfield that will be discussed in detail in the following section. Given that trauma-informed yoga is typically not included in a 200-hour YTT, most teachers will need to study it with someone with expertise and/or an appropriate yoga service organization.

Clinical Settings. Recommended credentials for teaching yoga in the V.A. and other clinical settings include:

- RYT 500 status, or equivalent training/experience;
- Training in military culture and communications, if needed;
- Training in trauma-informed yoga;
- At least five years teaching experience; and
- Additional specialized training as necessary to meet particular student needs, such as working with traumatic brain injuries (TBIs), chronic pain, and mobility impairments.

The level of training, experience, and maturity needed to teach yoga in the V.A. or another clinical setting is substantially higher than that required for physically fit, pre-deployment personnel. Programs administrators should be aware that finding yoga teachers with these qualifications may be challenging. Most likely, the best way to do so will be to contact a reputable organization that offers training in teaching yoga to veterans in your geographic area.[4] (In locales where in-person training is not available, online courses provide a valuable, if less then ideal, option.)

Community Settings. Teachers working with veterans in community settings such as VFWs, yoga studios, and nonprofit organizations should follow the guidelines listed for those serving pre-deployment personnel.

---

4 Promising ways to identify such organizations include conducting an online search (useful keywords: yoga, military, veterans, trauma, teacher, training, YTT, meditation, mindfulness), and contacting leading national organizations and asking for recommendations and guidance. Readers may also wish to consult the Contributor Bios Appendix to this volume to begin the process of familiarizing themselves with some of the leading organizations in the field.

STAFFING AND TRAINING 3: REQUIRE TEACHERS TO CARRY LIABILITY INSURANCE

Administrators should require yoga teachers working with military personnel to carry personal liability insurance.

Regardless of what type of insurance is carried by the organization hosting a class, yoga teachers should have their own liability insurance policy. This is standard in the field, and commonly required as a condition of certification and/or employment.

STAFFING AND TRAINING 4: CONSIDER PERSONAL CHARACTERISTICS

Consider how relevant personal characteristics of teachers including military experience, emotional maturity, and gender dynamics may impact their work with different groups of students.

Consider Military Experience. Some veterans believe that it is best to have veterans teach yoga to other veterans, if possible. Others feel that veteran or civilian status is not important; all that matters is quality of teaching. All agree that civilians can be excellent teachers. Some veterans, however, feel that there is a shared bond of experience among them that positively impacts students' experience in a unique way.

Notably, this latter perspective has support in the research literature. Hendricks Thomas and Plummer Taylor (2015), for example, contend that "warrior subculture creates a powerful mandate for peer-to-peer outreach." Their work suggests that if peer leadership has been proven an evidence-based best practice when it comes to analogous therapeutic work in similarly distinctive subcultures (e.g., peer mentoring to support recovery from addiction), having veterans teach yoga to other veterans is likely to be preferable as well.

Although the issue can be controversial, some veterans and military experts consequently believe that administrators seeking to hire yoga teachers should give preference to veterans. Such preferential employment practices, they argue, supports veterans as individuals, while providing valuable peer leadership to students. Hiring veteran yoga teachers is also seen as helping to root yoga more firmly in military culture.

It is commonly agreed that veteran teachers should not be considered exempt from the credentialing guidelines listed above, and that preferential hiring policies should never be allowed to compromise quality of teaching.

Prioritize Emotional Maturity. Emotional maturity does not necessarily correlate with age. Younger teachers may be more or less emotionally mature than their older counterparts, depending on the individuals involved. Irrespective of age, emotional maturity is always important in teaching yoga to veterans as it involves working with people who have been, or are prepared to be involved in extraordinarily challenging, often highly dangerous situations. It is particularly crucial in clinical settings.

Consider Gender Dynamics. With regard to hiring and staffing issues, key points to be aware of include:

- In keeping with the general demographics of the military, yoga classes for veterans will typically be heavily weighted toward men. Female teachers working with majority male classes must have the maturity to remain centered and non-reactive when confronted with sexual innuendo and banter, as well as the confidence to draw appropriate lines of acceptable behavior as necessary.
- If classes are restricted to one gender (typically, women-only), they should be staffed by a teacher of the same gender.
- Teachers should be sensitized to the needs and concerns of LGBTQ students, and committed to learning more about these issues as necessary.

For a more in-depth discussion of these issues, see the "Best Practices: Gender Considerations" section.

STAFFING AND TRAINING 5: HAVE SUBSTITUTE TEACHERS AVAILABLE

Classes in clinical settings should have substitute teachers trained and available.

Although it is useful for any yoga class to have substitute teachers who have first-hand experience with the class available, it is particularly important for veterans in clinical settings (or anywhere in which a high proportion of students may have experienced trauma). As will be discussed in the following section, trauma-informed yoga classes are designed to provide students with an experience of safety, predictability, and control. Cancelling classes, or switching from a known to an unknown teacher, disrupts this foundation and should be avoided if possible.

Ideally, teachers working in clinical settings should arrange to have substitute teachers come to class, be introduced to students, and co-teach part of the session. In some cases, this will not be allowed due to privacy regulations. Teachers should be familiar with relevant policies, and figure out how best to work within their guidelines to prepare students and subs alike to become as comfortable with each other as possible.

In some cases, staffing limitations may make it difficult to have substitute teachers available. VA administrators and others charged with staffing clinical programs should consider how to address the need for substitute teachers given their staffing and resource constraints carefully. Although periodically canceling classes may seem trivial, doing so negatively impacts their accrued therapeutic benefit by undercutting whatever foundation of interpersonal trust, programmatic reliability, and positive habit formation has been built.

STAFFING AND TRAINING 6: CONSIDER TEACHER COMPENSATION CAREFULLY

Program providers should carefully weigh the pros and cons of staffing classes with paid, as opposed to volunteer teachers.

The question to whether to staff programs with paid or volunteer teachers is critical and requires careful consideration. Some providers feel strongly that in order to assure program stability, it is crucial for yoga teachers to be paid staff, rather than volunteers. Others believe that it is possible to build a strong program with volunteer staff.

Of course, the resources available to pay teachers will vary among providers. Decisions regarding compensation should be made after considering both immediate and long-term program needs. Even if a program does not have the funding to pay teachers in the short run, program providers should consider whether lasting stability and quality can be maintained while relying on volunteers.

The issue of teacher compensation is particularly critical in clinical settings, where higher levels of training and experience are required. Hiring under-qualified teachers could negatively impact program quality—which, in turn, could have a negative impact on students' physical, psychological, and emotional safety and well-being. In some cases, it may be difficult to find volunteers with the qualifications to teach yoga in clinical settings. In such cases, it is recommended to hold off on beginning the program until this problem is addressed.

BEST PRACTICES FOR WORKING WITH TRAUMA

As noted in the "Staffing and Training" section, yoga teachers working with military personnel should have had specialized training in trauma-informed yoga (TIY) before beginning to teach. This recommendation is all-inclusive and encompasses teachers working with personnel who are on and off active duty, pre- and post-deployment, and able-bodied and disabled. The one exception to this rule would be yoga teachers who are also mental health professionals. If they have prior training in trauma and are comfortable integrating that knowledge into their yoga instruction, there is no need for additional specialized training.

This recommendation is not based on the assumption that military personnel have commonly experienced trauma. Rather, it's recommended because: 1) TIY is based on scientific theories that are important for all yoga instructors to know but are not yet standard in the field; and 2) yoga teachers should be prepared to work with students who are grappling with PTSD (Post-Traumatic Stress Disorder), as well as related issues such as anxiety, depression, or moral injury.[5] While recommended for all teachers, TIY training is especially critical for those working in the VA and other clinical settings.

---

5 While not the same as PTSD, the symptoms of moral injury commonly look quite similar. See Wood (2014).

WORKING WITH TRAUMA 1: UNDERSTAND TRAUMA-INFORMED YOGA

Yoga teachers working with veterans should understand the scientific and theoretical bases of trauma-informed yoga.

The theory, teaching, and practice of trauma-informed yoga are relatively new. David Emerson, a yoga teacher who works closely with Dr. Bessel van der Kolk, MD, an internationally recognized leader in the field of psychological trauma, first coined the term "trauma-sensitive yoga" in 2002.[6] Based at the Trauma Center at the Justice Resource Center in Massachusetts, Emerson and van der Kolk have remained at the forefront of a rapidly growing movement to incorporate yoga into therapeutic programs for PTSD (Emerson and Hopper 2011, van der Kolk 2014). Their work has also been used to inform therapeutic yoga programming for a range of issues including addiction recovery, eating disorders, sexual violence, and more.

Insights and techniques developed for trauma-informed yoga are beginning to influence the teaching and practice of yoga more generally. A new wave of critical reflection and discussion has recently developed among yoga professionals in the wake of highly publicized reports of physical injuries, unhealthy psychological dynamics, and other problems in the field. As formerly taken-for-granted norms and methods are being questioned, trauma-informed yoga has emerged as a valuable resource to learn from among teachers dedicated to offering classes that are both physically and psychologically safe, healing, and empowering.

Theory of Trauma. Trauma-informed yoga is based on a particular understanding of trauma, one that emphasizes its impact on the entire mind-body system, as opposed to particular mental states (e.g., troubling memories) viewed in isolation from the physical body. "Trauma," van der Kolk (2014) explains, "is not

6 Although this discussion is indebted to Emerson and Hopper (2011) and van der Kolk's (2014) work, we use the term "trauma-informed" as opposed to "trauma-sensitive" yoga to indicate our reliance on additional sources, some of which may advocate slightly different yoga teaching methods.

just an event that took place sometime in the past; it is also the imprint left by that experience on mind, brain, and body" (21). Drawing from neuroscience, developmental psychology, and interpersonal neurobiology, this view of trauma considers body-based therapeutic methods, such as trauma-informed yoga and EMDR,[7] to be of at least co-equal importance to more traditional ones, such as talk therapy.

Traumatic events involve "inescapable shock": threats to physical survival and/or psycho-emotional integrity experienced in circumstances that prevent safe escape. Traumatic events may be one-time occurrences, such as a car crash, or part of an ongoing pattern, such as chronic domestic violence. Though single-event PTSD and complex, developmental trauma differ, both evoke a nervous system response that involves the body's instinctual fight/flight/freeze pattern, which is hardwired into the human nervous system to help protect us from harm. Normally, this provides the energy needed to propel us to safety. Trauma occurs when we are unable to take effective action to stay safe, and remain trapped in a physically threatening and/or psychologically overwhelming situation.

Hyper- and Hypo-Arousal. If we do not consequently have the opportunity to process and release the resultant sense of shock experienced throughout the body-mind system, we may remain stuck in a state of severe physiological and psycho-emotional disequilibrium. Often, this manifests as hyper- or hypo-arousal.

To be hyper-aroused is to remain in a hyper-vigilant state of "high alert" regardless of actual circumstance, acutely anxious and obsessively scanning the environment for potential threats. Conversely, hypo-arousal is a state of being "shut down," feeling lethargic, apathetic, depressed, disassociated, or otherwise numbly disconnected from life.

Either way, "traumatized people chronically feel unsafe inside their bodies. The past is alive in the form of gnawing interior discomfort" (ibid., 96). This chronic

---

7 EMDR, or Eye Movement Desensitization and Reprocessing, is a therapeutic technique that many have found highly effective in training trauma. See van der Kolk (2014), Chap. 15.

sense of dis-ease commonly produces or exacerbates additional problems, such as substance abuse, disrupted relationships, and excessive or even dangerous over-reactions to otherwise minor events. Over the long term, chronic stress and/or unaddressed PTSD may cause other serious health problems, including cardiovascular disease and diabetes.

In addition to finding ways to discharge incomplete impulses related to nervous system activation, an important part of trauma recovery is to support survivors in recognizing and responding healthfully to their current physiological/psychological state. When taught and learned from a trauma-informed perspective, yoga can be a vitally helpful resource on each of these fronts.

Yoga can have both stimulating and soothing effects. This is true on both the physical and psycho-emotional levels. Yoga teachers can encourage balance in the nervous system through classes that incorporate both stimulating and soothing postures, and by encouraging students to notice when they feel safe, soothed and secure. Part of the skill of a trauma-informed teacher is to emphasize present-state awareness and offer opportunities for students to choose what brings them balance. Over time, students can build coping skills and make choices that support their transition from hyper- or hypo-arousal to a balanced state (Danylchuk, 2015).

"Triggers." Overly intensive reactions to more or less everyday events (e.g., unexpected loud noises) are popularly referred to as "triggers."[8] It is important for yoga teachers working with veterans to understand that "being triggered" is part of the pattern of physiological disequilibrium produced by traumatic experience. Yoga instructors working with veterans in clinical settings need to know why and how to adapt standard teaching practices to minimize potential triggers.

It should be emphasized that the practice of yoga may at times be triggering for some students no matter how highly trained and experienced the teacher.

---

8 As the term "trigger" is increasingly being used in other areas of American culture, its meaning is becoming more confusing, and even contentious (e.g., controversies over whether college professors should label selected assigned readings with "trigger warnings"). This popular usage is only loosely related to the clinically rooted understanding of the term used here.

For this reason, teachers working with students suffering from PTSD should always have solid working relationships with support staff and clinicians (see "Relationship Building Best Practices," below).[9]

Complementary Therapies. Understood as an experience that disrupts the mind-body system, unwinding the physiological and psychological patterns encoded by trauma may require a combination of: 1) "top-down," cognitive-based talk therapies to help process memories, strengthen relationships, and develop meaningful personal narratives; 2) "bottom-up," body-based therapies to help calm down the nervous system, self-regulate, and feel and tolerate a range of emotions and sensations; and 3) if needed, taking medications under the supervision of a qualified professional to provide the foundation necessary for cognitive- and body-based therapies to be effective (ibid., 3).

Trauma-informed yoga and EMDR are widely considered to be the most effective body-based therapies available. It is critical to realize that yoga will be most effective in healing trauma when it is integrated into a larger set of therapeutic supports that have been specifically tailored to the individual. Teachers should never lead students to believe that yoga is a stand-alone therapy. Even if yoga is the only therapeutic modality that a student wants to engage with, teachers should communicate that it's always best to remain open to complementary therapies, resources, and supports.

WORKING WITH TRAUMA 2: ADAPT TIY PRINCIPLES TO MILITARY CONTEXT

Consider how trauma-informed yoga principles can be adapted to inform teaching dedicated to building resilience and countering military stressors more generally.

---

9 The re-experiencing of intensive feelings of physical and psychological distress associated with traumatic experience may or may not be sparked by an identifiable trigger; symptoms such as nightmares, intrusive thoughts, and flashbacks frequently arise without it. For a helpful discussion of the "cycle of stress" that includes hyper- and hypo-arousal and re-experiencing, as well as guidance on how to help alleviate this cycle with yoga, see Manafort and Gilmartin (2013).

The benefits of trauma-informed yoga can and commonly do extend well beyond the boundaries of teaching students suffering from clinical trauma. For yoga teachers working with veterans, it is useful to consider how the insights into the mind-body relationship that inform TIY can be applied to the experience of coping with common military stressors more generally.

For example, military training and combat can lead to a state of heightened awareness and increased sympathetic nervous system firing whether trauma is experienced or not. In the short term, this hyper-arousal can be an adaptive response, increasing physical abilities that may be needed in combat or countering physical threats. However, some individuals may remain in a hyper-aroused state in a post-military, civilian environment. This excess sympathetic response can produce imbalances in the nervous system, leading to anxiety, depression, irritability, hypertension, insomnia, and other problems.

For many veterans, the relationship between the mind and body has been fractured after years of disciplining the body and overriding or compartmentalizing thoughts and feelings as necessary to put the mission first. An appropriately designed yoga class provides an opportunity to reconnect body and mind by developing new skills of proprioception (internal awareness of the physical body), interoception (internal awareness of feelings and sensations), self-regulation,[10] and present-moment awareness. Over time, these resources support successful reintegration into civilian life.[11]

10 In this book, "self-regulation" is understood as the ability to be aware of our own thoughts, feelings, and behaviors, and to work with them in healthy, considerate, and socially responsible ways. As such, self-regulation exists on a spectrum of greater and lesser degrees of self-awareness and healthy self-management: If no human being is ever perfectly self-regulated, it is certainly possible to be significantly more or less aware of one's own negative thoughts, emotions, and behaviors, and to have greater and lesser tools and resources available for managing them appropriately.

11 Conversely, yoga class can also be designed to build resilience among pre-deployment personnel, ideally reducing the incidence of PTSD and smoothing transitions back to civilian life down the road. For information on the growing interest in yoga and mindfulness as resilience-building resources for pre-deployment personnel, see Hendricks Thomas and Plummer Taylor (2016).

WORKING WITH TRAUMA 3: MAXIMIZE SAFETY, PREDICTABILITY, AND CONTROL

Yoga teachers should strive to create and maintain a classroom environment that maximizes a shared sense of safety, predictability, and control.

Teaching yoga in ways that maximize a shared sense of safety, predictability, and control is a cornerstone of trauma-informed yoga. As such, it is particularly important for teachers working with veterans in clinical settings, or other contexts in which students with PTSD may be present. As noted above, however, TIY principles are useful even in cases where students may not have experienced trauma, but may be grappling with related issues such as anxiety, depression, or moral injury.

For students with PTSD, a sense of safety, predictability, and control helps to unwind the physiological and psychological impact of traumatic experience, which is generally unsafe, unpredictable, and out of one's individual control. In working with veterans more generally, these qualities can provide a counterweight to the eroded ability to trust the environment, and even one's deeper sense of self, that can develop in response to the unpredictable contexts of war, combat, and other military experiences.

Specific ways of setting up the classroom and giving instruction that support a shared sense of safety, predictability, and control are detailed in the "Teaching and Curriculum Best Practices II: Teacher and Classroom Prep" section.

WORKING WITH TRAUMA 4: PRACTICE TOGETHER

Teachers should integrate instruction with practicing with students; any additional movement should be intentional, predictable, and minimal.

In many yoga classes, it is standard for the teacher to rely almost entirely on verbal instruction, physically demonstrating only a few poses or techniques throughout the course of a class. It is also common for teachers to walk around the class while talking so that they can see what students are doing, and adapt their instructions accordingly.

Generally speaking, this common approach to yoga instruction is not recommended for students with trauma. Having the teacher walk around the room with no predictable course of movement, and looking at students from unpredictable angles, may be disruptive to students, possibly over-stimulating their nervous systems and putting them on "high alert." As such, it undermines the overarching goal of creating an environment that maximizes students' sense of safety, predictability, and control.

Consequently, it is recommended that TIY teachers try as much as possible to teach from one spot in the room, combining verbal instruction with an ongoing demonstration of poses—in other words, "practicing together." When teachers need to move to different places in the room, they should announce what they are doing, and why: e.g., "I'm going to go to the window side of the room now so that everyone can see me."

Any time a teacher feels that it is best to change physical locations, it is recommended that he or she move in mindful, deliberate ways that maintain a sense of predictability for students. Going slowly enough so that students can visually track the teacher's movements easily also tends to be calming to the nervous system.

WORKING WITH TRAUMA 5: USE INVITATIONAL LANGUAGE

Teach yoga using language that invites rather than commands, and provides opportunities for students to make choices concerning how to engage with the practice.

Instruction in yoga classes is often given as a series of commands (e.g., "Close your eyes. Deepen your breath. Inhale and lengthen your spine"). This is not recommended in trauma-informed yoga. Instead, teachers should use wording that invites engagement and provides simple choices (e.g., "if you would like to close your eyes, feel free; if not, then soften your gaze"). This approach helps counteract the experience of trauma, which involves losing the power to choose to take action to be safe. It can also help re-socialize veterans to the new "mission" of tuning in with how they are feeling in the present moment, and taking action that supports their own personal health and well-being.

Simple choices that can be built into the structure of a yoga class include which mat to choose, whether to use a prop, which variation of a pose to practice, and how long to hold a position. Rather than give students "permission" to do something, teachers should communicate that everything is "optional," including all poses, use of props, eyes open or closed, etc.

Count-Down Cues. When initiating a posture, clearly stating the *suggested* length of the pose (e.g. five breaths) and giving permission to come out of any poses as needed can help students avoid feeling stuck or trapped. Also, "counting down" the suggested time frame (e.g., "holding, if you like, for 5 . . . 4 . . . 3 . . . 2 . . . 1") provides both a predictable framework, and the opportunity to make appropriate personal choices within it. Again, using invitational, rather than commanding language helps create a healing setting in which students can learn to respond appropriately to their own internal sensations, rather than ignore or numb them.

WORKING WITH TRAUMA 6: AVOID PSYCHOLOGICALLY DISCOMFORTING POSES

Be extremely conservative in teaching poses likely to carry sexual connotations; monitor the emotional energy of the class, and adjust accordingly.

When teaching trauma-informed yoga, it is critical to be aware that some poses are more likely to carry sexual connotations for students than others (e.g., postures that overtly expose the genital area, such as happy baby or reclining cobbler). As a general rule, such poses should not be taught. The exception would be in cases where the teacher has worked with the individual students long enough to believe that introducing them would be truly therapeutic. Given that these situations will be rare, the best course of action is to avoid them.

Teachers should keep in mind that some poses may be psychologically discomforting or even triggering for students in ways that are unpredictable, and difficult to foresee. Consequently, teachers should strive to monitor the emotional energy of the class, and make adjustments to the lesson plan as needed. For example, if it seems that students are becoming frustrated in their attempts to keep up with the class, instruction should be immediately adjusted in ways that will hopefully re-establish a greater sense of ease (e.g., slowing down the pace, or shifting to less physically challenging postures).

That said, there are times when yoga will prove discomforting—or even triggering—to students no matter what the teacher's level of skill and sensitivity.

Psychological discomfort is not necessarily a problem, provided that students can simultaneously maintain a sense of grounding, centering, safety, and calm. Over time, it becomes easier for many yoga practitioners to experience the rise and fall of psychological and emotional discomfort while retaining a sense of inner peace. This experience can be deeply healing. It also, however, represents a more advanced way of practicing yoga. As such, teachers should not presume it is accessible to all students, particularly beginners.

If a student is triggered, this may or may not be evident to the teacher. Ideally, teachers should have a protocol developed for cases in which a student may require immediate support. It is helpful and important to become knowledgeable about trauma, develop solid relationships with students, and be cautious with discomforting poses and sequencing. However, this cannot guarantee that triggering will never occur.

WORKING WITH TRAUMA 7: BE CONSERVATIVE IN USE OF TOUCH

As a general rule, yoga teachers should avoid touching students.

In many yoga classes, it is standard practice for teachers to give physical "adjustments" or "assists" in poses. Typically, this means that the teacher places their hands on students in ways intended to guide them into an enhanced experience of a pose (e.g., safer physical alignment, or a deeper stretch). This otherwise common practice is not recommended for trauma-informed classes.

As a general rule, any sort of touch, including "adjustments," is avoided in TIY. The unpredictability of being touched by the teacher undermines students' general sense of safety, predictably, and control. Although it is possible for teachers to ask for verbal consent before touching students, it is generally difficult for them to say "no" unless a strong prior relationship has been established. This is generally impossible in a standard yoga setting.

Having the boundary of physical touch crossed can feel invasive, and undermine students' sense of control over their own bodies. For those who have experienced physical and/or sexual abuse, this can be troubling or even triggering.

That said, there are some circumstances under which touch can be experienced as helpful and healing. These are generally limited to cases in which the teacher has received specialized training in the use of touch in TIY, and is working in a setting that supports this specialized protocol. Otherwise, it is generally best to avoid touching students and rely on verbal instruction instead.

WORKING WITH TRAUMA 8: DON'T ASSUME OR COMPARE

Teachers should never assume that veterans have or have not experienced trauma; civilians should refrain from comparing veterans' experiences with their own lives.

Yoga teachers should be careful never to make assumptions about their students' experiences, whether regarding trauma or more generally. Civilian teachers in particular should remember that many veterans who have experienced combat or other highly dangerous situations were not traumatized by it, and have never suffered from PTSD.

Yoga teachers should also be aware that military members who have experienced trauma (whether in the service, their family of origin, or elsewhere) may be resistant to labeling it as such. Consequently, while it is critical to understand trauma and be prepared to work with it, teachers should neither assume its existence, nor discuss it in ways that may be inadvertently alienating to veterans.

Yoga teachers should also refrain from comparing the challenges of civilian life to those experienced in the military. Even if a civilian teacher has experienced trauma, veterans may be put off by any assumption of equivalence with what they were exposed to in the military. There may be exceptions to this general rule, but it is best to follow it except in situations where strong relationships between teacher and students already exist.

WORKING WITH TRAUMA 9: UTILIZE A STRENGTHS-BASED MODEL

Teach from a strengths-based perspective that supports post-traumatic growth.

Yoga teachers working with students with trauma should employ a strengths-based, rather than deficit-oriented model. Teachers working with veterans should commit to doing the background work and training necessary to enable teaching yoga in ways that prioritize resilience and post-traumatic growth.[12]

12 For a general discussion of post-traumatic growth, see Tedeschi and Calhoun (2004). For teaching yoga for resilience and post-traumatic growth in the context of military culture, see Hendricks Thomas (2015).

TEACHING AND CURRICULUM BEST PRACTICES

Teaching yoga is not a mechanistic endeavor. Different teachers will be drawn to different methods. Even within a given method, they will interpret and embody the teachings differently. To a large extent, this is how it should be. Yoga works best when the teacher has a deeply personal connection to the practice, yet is also adept at transmitting it to others in ways that are appropriate to them.

While this book presents guidelines and recommendations, it does not attempt to provide detailed class plans or instructions for specific poses. Instead, it focuses on yoga teaching and curriculum issues that can be applied to a variety of different methods, ranging from physically vigorous to gentle or adaptive. Because this is such a large topic, this set of Best Practices is divided into the four subcategories of: 1) General Guidelines, 2) Teacher and Class Prep, 3) Instructional Basics, and 4) Teaching Self-Regulation Skills. Readers should note that complementary recommendations for working with specific populations and/or in particular contexts are integrated into other sections (e.g., working with trauma, classes for military and veteran families, teaching in the VA).

TEACHING AND CURRICULUM I: GENERAL GUIDELINES

GENERAL GUIDELINES 1: Teach Mindful Yoga

Teach yoga as practice of integrating mind, movement, and breath, adapted as necessary to meet individual and group needs.

As the popularity of yoga has exploded in the U.S. and worldwide, it has become increasingly absorbed into fitness culture. Traditionally, however, yoga was never meant to be simply exercise. Of course, it can be taught and practiced in ways that provide an excellent workout. That should only be done, however, in cases where it is the most effective means of teaching students to integrate mind, movement, and breath.

Teachers should have the ability to adapt the practice as necessary to meet the needs of the individuals and groups they are working with. In some cases, a physically challenging practice will be appropriate; in others, it won't. There is no one-size-fits-all way to design an effective class. Regardless of the level of physical challenge, however, it is always important to prioritize teaching students to work with their mental focus and breath.

GENERAL GUIDELINES 2: Maintain Professional Boundaries

Yoga teachers should understand the boundaries of their professional role, and remain clearly within them at all times.

Yoga teachers must be sufficiently self-aware to consistently maintain professional boundaries with students, program administrators, and staff. Even those who have clinical licensing must remain aware that if they are employed as yoga teachers, they are not to play the role of an ad hoc therapist. Similarly, teachers should refrain from serving as informal physical therapists or medical advisors.

Yoga teachers should also do the work necessary to uproot any personal issues that might cause them to present yoga as some sort of cure-all or silver bullet. Such attitudes are common in certain corners of yoga culture and should be scrupulously avoided.

As a general rule, it is recommended that yoga teachers working in the VA do not socialize with veteran students except in the context of officially sanctioned events such as VA picnics, socials, and program graduations. In all cases, yoga teachers should avoid personal relationships with students that have (or might be construed to have) romantic and/or sexual dimensions.

GENERAL GUIDELINES 3: Respect Secular Values

Teach yoga in a way that respects secular values and maintains its integrity as a holistic practice.

Yoga teachers should be mindful that common elements of North American yoga culture may carry religious connotations for some students. Regardless of their own beliefs or what works best in their own personal practice, yoga teachers working with veterans should commit to teaching yoga in strictly secular ways. This requires being mindful of any religious connotations of language used in class, as well as non-verbal elements such as music, bells, chimes, and chanting.

Teachers should not teach yoga philosophy except in evidently secularized forms. They should reflect on whether they have any sort of personal agenda dedicated to converting students to becoming yogis, or convincing them of the veracity of yoga philosophy. If so, they need to do the personal work necessary to resist these tendencies. Put differently, yoga teachers should reflect honestly on whether they harbor an "inner evangelist," and, if so, make sure to keep this tendency in check.

In order to be equally welcoming to students of all faiths or none, it is recommended to avoid chants of any type, including the commonly practiced syllable "Om." Yoga teachers should also consider minimizing or eliminating the use of Sanskrit, which is commonly used to name poses in many civilian classes. Many

Hindus consider Sanskrit to be a sacred language (similar to the traditional status of Latin in Catholicism). Also, military personnel who were deployed in the Middle East may find that it reminds them of Arabic, an association which could prove distracting or triggering.

Teachers may still wish to end class with the word "Namaste," which has become traditional in North American yoga culture. This provides a nice opportunity to honor yoga's roots in Indian civilization without invoking a particular religious tradition.[13] However, teachers should provide a secular translation of the term to students in English, and be prepared to provide simple answers to student questions about yoga's relationship to religion and/or Indian culture. In so doing, they should be prepared to knowledgeably communicate a sense of respect and appreciation for the history, culture, and religions of India, as the land in which yoga was originally rooted, and subsequently modernized and developed.[14]

Teaching a secular class does not require eviscerating yoga's potential as a holistic "mind-body-spirit" practice (Horton 2016). Yoga can and should still be taught and experienced as a practice that offers more than simply exercise—or even therapy. However, doing so requires invoking the "spirit" part of the "mind-body-spirit" equation only in ways that are commonly accepted as secular.

For example, yoga can help to "uplift the human spirit" by sparking the creative synergy of our natural mind-body communication processes. There is nothing religious or metaphysical in such a perspective. In fact, a growing body of scientific research supports the underlying claim that developing skills such as interoception and metacognition through yoga or similar practices can profoundly enrich quality of life (Schmalzl et al, 2015).

---

13 While "Namaste" literally translates as "I bow to you," in Indian culture it's the equivalent of a respectful "Hello" in the English-speaking world.

14 The history and development of yoga is a vast, and sometimes controversial topic. Foundational reference works on this subject include Feuerstein (2001), Singleton (2010), and Mallinson and Singleton (forthcoming, 2016).

TEACHING AND CURRICULUM 2: TEACHER AND CLASS PREP

TEACHER AND CLASS PREP 1: Prepare the Classroom Environment

Yoga teachers should carefully prepare the classroom or teaching space prior to student arrival.

Yoga classes for veterans may take place in a wide variety of settings: traditional yoga studios, gyms on military installations, meeting rooms in community organizations, makeshift spaces in the VA, etc. As a result, it is not always possible to control key elements of the class environment, such as temperature, noise level, furnishings, and so on. In all cases, yoga teachers should carefully consider how to work best within the limitations of the space available, and arrive early enough before class starts to create the best teaching environment possible.

Furnishings. When teaching in non-traditional spaces not designed for yoga classes, it may be necessary to move furniture in order to create space for the class. Yoga teachers should work with building administrators and staff to develop a shared understanding about how best to arrange the space, and who will be responsible for moving furniture as needed.

In cases where building staff have agreed to set up the room, teachers should still arrive early enough to do it themselves if warranted, at least until a consistent pattern of room readiness has been established. Particularly in understaffed or otherwise demanding environments, staff may not always be available to set up the room as planned due to last-minute contingencies. If staff are not available and teachers cannot ready the room alone, they should consider whether it is possible—and appropriate—to enlist student help as necessary to set up the room for class. This should be discussed with building administrators in advance.

Finally, yoga teachers should have a clear understanding of what, if anything, is expected of them in terms of reconfiguring the room once class is over, and be sure that they have the capacity to follow through as needed.

Cleanliness. Like furnishings, cleanliness tends to be more of an issue when teaching in non-traditional, makeshift spaces. Yoga teachers should work with building administrators as needed to make sure that their teaching space is as clean as possible.

Teachers working in understaffed or otherwise challenging settings should be prepared to do some light cleaning themselves as necessary. This will most likely require working with building administrators to ensure access to, for example, a broom and dustpan on site. Since this will not always be possible, teachers working in such environments must be mentally prepared to do excellent work regardless of the quality (or lack thereof) of the space available.

Temperature and Ventilation. Having the room at a comfortable temperature and sufficiently ventilated is an important component of the classroom environment. Teachers should know the full range of standard and default options available, such as access to thermostats, space heaters, fans, windows, etc. Teachers working in non-traditional settings may have to adjust to less than optimal circumstances. For example, dressing in layers may be necessary to teach in cold rooms whose temperature can't be adjusted.

Lighting. Lighting is an important component of the classroom environment, and options should be carefully considered prior to launching a new class. In some cases, it won't be possible to control the lighting at all. In most, however, there will at least be a few alternatives available.

Choosing the best option can be tricky, as different students have different needs and preferences. Some veterans prefer bright lighting because it promotes awareness. Others may find it difficult to relax sufficiently without it, as dim lighting can cause some veterans to "go on alert" in response to not being able to see their environment clearly. Such a reaction is particularly likely among veterans with PTSD. Consequently, when teaching in environments where there may be a high proportion of students with trauma, dim lighting should either be avoided or used with caution.

Some veterans, however, like dim lighting because it is conducive to relaxation. Notably, this may be true even among students who have experienced trauma. While generalizations can be made about particular patterns, there is no one-size-fits-all answer to the question of what lighting option works best.

Consequently, when making decisions about lighting, teachers should carefully consider who is in the class and how lighting may affect those particular students. In some cases, it may work best for teachers to show students two or three simple options before class starts, and ask what they prefer. Once a decision about lighting has been made, it's best to announce to students that it will remain consistent throughout the class series.

Spatial Awareness. For students with PTSD or otherwise grappling with hyper-vigilance, knowing where the door, exits, windows, and bathrooms are located can be important in creating a sense of safety. With this in mind, teachers should familiarize themselves with their teaching space prior to their first class.

In the process, it's important to strategize about how best to position themselves as teachers, as well as their students, for class. Teachers should have a specific mat configuration in mind before class beings, and arrive in time to make sure that mats are set up accordingly. Once a good mat configuration is determined, it should remain consistent from class to class.

In most cases, it's best to arrange mats so that the teacher is positioned near the main entry/exit door, so that he or she is able to monitor and, at least to some extent, control it. This puts the teacher in a good position to call for help if needed, which is important for everyone's safety. It also means that he or she will know if students or others are entering or exiting the class.

Student mats should be positioned so that students will have a clear view of both the teacher and the main door. When possible, position student mats so that there is ample space between them. Ideally, everyone should feel that they have sufficient personal space. Students may also feel safer when they can practice yoga with no one behind them. In cases where this is not possible, mats should be staggered in ways that minimize the sense of having another person right behind one's back.

To support student choice and control, it is best to allow them to pick out their own mats and mat space when possible, while maintaining the preset configuration of the room.

Yoga Props. Chairs, blocks, bolsters, blankets, and straps have become commonplace in many yoga classes. Teachers should consider what is accessible and appropriate, and teach prop usage in accordance with their training. They should also make sure that students have all necessary props near them at the beginning of class to allow easy access as needed.

Non-traditional class spaces may have no props available. If there is a budget that could be used to purchase props, teachers should prioritize based on student needs. If props cannot be purchased, teachers should find out if chairs are available (most clinical settings will have them) and request the proper number in advance.

As a general rule, it's good to have chairs available for balancing postures, and to support physical stability as needed. Students who are not comfortable on a mat may prefer to begin class in a chair and migrate to the mat if and when they feel comfortable. Some students may need to move back and forth between chair and mat throughout the course of the class. Teachers should encourage everyone who might benefit from this option to exercise it.

Music. Some students experience music during class as a positive resource that assists them with focus and relaxation. Others, however, may find it distracting or even triggering. Consequently, it's important that yoga teachers who wish to play music in class choose it with care.

There is no one-size-fits-all answer to the question of what type of music works best. Recommendations from experienced teachers vary. Some believe that instrumental selections are best, as words may shift students' focus too much "into their heads" and/or carry problematic emotional connotations. Others report that words can be helpful to students with PTSD, as they provide a focal point for the mind that helps prevent traumatic memories and sensations from resurfacing in destabilizing ways. All agree that if songs with words are played, the content should be screened carefully to make sure that only positive, secular messages are conveyed.

Similarly, some teachers hold that popular, "Top 40"-type are best avoided, as they may spark memories and carry emotional baggage. Others, however, have found that playing popular music makes yoga feel more accessible to military personnel by connecting it with something so culturally familiar. All agree that while popular music may work well in classes at military installations, it is not recommended for clinical settings.

In all cases, music that reminds veterans of their service experience should be avoided, particularly anything reminiscent of places where they may have been stationed. By the same token, it is best to avoid music that includes chanting, or unfamiliar languages or sounds.

TEACHER AND CLASS PREP 2: Arrive Prepared to Teach

Yoga teachers should arrive physically, psychologically, and emotionally prepared to teach.

Arriving prepared to teach each and every class requires background preparation and ongoing work. Some aspects of being prepared are relatively simple, such as understanding how to dress and why. Others, however, are more complex, and require personal work on the part of the teacher. For example, being able to maintain appropriate professional boundaries requires not simply understanding technical roles, but also being aware of more subtle personal and interpersonal dynamics.

Because yoga is most effective as a holistic mind-body integration practice—as opposed to simply a form of exercise or therapy—teachers need to "do their own work" in the form of study and training, as well as ongoing self-reflection and self-care in order to show up most effectively for their students. Particularly important aspects of teacher preparation to consider are detailed below.

Dress Appropriately. Yoga teachers working with service members should avoid wearing clothing that may be sexually suggestive or otherwise distracting to students, such as low necklines, leggings, tank tops, or tight muscle shirts. Modest yoga clothing or comfortable street wear is best. Loose, comfortable clothing with no bare skin is the appropriate attire for a therapeutic teacher. T-shirts with logos, political views, or lifestyle choices should be avoided, as they may have problematic associations for students, and/or cause real or perceived divisions between them and the teacher.

Avoid Scents. Yoga teachers should avoid wearing scents to class, as some students may be highly sensitive to them. Scents can also trigger disturbing memories or feelings for students suffering from acute anxiety or PTSD. These cautions apply to strongly scented personal care products, perfumes, and essential oils.

Respect Punctuality and Order. Military personnel appreciate punctuality. A well-known saying in military circles is, "*If you show up on time, you are late.*" In keeping with this ethos, and to support a shared sense of safety, predictability, and control, it is important that yoga teachers start and end classes on time. Punctuality is also critical in the VA and other clinical settings, where the room used for yoga will most likely be scheduled to accommodate other needs before and after class.

If there is a particular sequence or order to a class or workshop, teachers should try to stay with it. Changing things last minute, or creating a general sense of unpredictability may cause unease and discomfort.

TEACHER AND CLASS PREP 3: Orient Students to Class

Before commencing with formal instruction, yoga teachers should briefly introduce themselves, and orient students to the physical environment and class structure.

It is important for teachers to gain and maintain student trust. One way to help with this is to provide a clear, concise introduction to the class. When beginning a new session, yoga teachers should explain who they are, what they do, and why they teach yoga. They should also maintain a professional, respectful, confident, and authentic demeanor.

It can be helpful for teachers to give students a basic outline or roadmap of each class before starting. For example, a brief review of class content and length helps students know what to expect. Teachers may also wish to explain that yoga is a practice of increasing self-empowerment, and remind students that they always have the option to slow down or rest.

Teachers should also provide ground rules to students as necessary to support classroom management and structure. Clear boundaries to keep might include appropriate attire, timeliness, respect for others, and so on. Additional points to consider are elaborated below.

Orient to the Room. Some members of the military are trained to check closets and doorways to determine potential threats. If this is a common practice for students, teachers should allow them to do it, as it can enhance their ability to settle into the room and feel safe.

Teachers can further support a shared sense of safety and predictability by orienting students to their surroundings more generally: e.g., saying, "*Look around the room as we begin and notice the details of this room, this space that we are coming together in.*" Students should also always be given the option to practice with their eyes open or closed throughout class.

Teachers may wish to verbalize that they are providing a secure environment. In so doing, it is helpful to include sensory detail, e.g.: "*My eyes will be open the whole time in this class,*" "The *exits to the room are behind me,*" or "*Noises or other unexpected interruptions may occur during class.*" Teachers should be mindful to never make any promises they can't keep, however small (e.g., don't say that your eyes will always be open if you have an ingrained habit of closing them at certain times, as you may slip up).

Teachers should take care to acknowledge any potential distractions or unexpected sounds that may occur during class (e.g., a noise-generating change in the heating or cooling system, or an intercom announcement). This helps establish a sense of group comfort and predictability around sensory input. At the same time, it supports student confidence in the teacher by indicating an awareness of what's happening, and a readiness to address whatever unexpected issues may arise.

Open-Door Policy. An explicitly stated open-door policy—giving students the option to exit and enter the room as needed—is recommended unless class circumstances make it impossible (e.g., teaching in a jail or prison). This helps reinforce students' sense of control and encourages them to take responsibility for their own experience.

Manage Cell Phones. It is recommended that teachers ask students to set their phones to "airplane mode." In circumstances where a cell phone ring or vibration would be excessively disruptive, teachers may need to ask students to leave them outside the room. They should understand, however, that it can be difficult for veterans to attend class, and that they may need to be reachable for family emergencies or other issues. The need to avoid the disruption of phone alerts must be balanced with student needs. Teachers should work with students to manage phones for the good of the group, and avoid harsh behavior or shaming comments if they do prove disruptive.

TEACHING AND CURRICULUM 3: INSTRUCTIONAL BASICS

INSTRUCTIONAL BASICS 1: Sequence Carefully

Sequence in a way that minimizes risks of injury, stress, and anxiety, and maximizes opportunities to practice internal awareness, deep relaxation, and self-regulation.

The sequence in which different yoga postures, breath work, and mindfulness exercises are presented is critical to how they are experienced, both physiologically and psychologically. For example, teaching an intense backbend toward the end of class, after students have been sufficiently warmed up, can be healing and exhilarating. Teaching the same pose too early in class, however, could easily cause injury.

The same principle holds true for breath work and mindfulness exercises. What may be deeply relaxing when properly sequenced could cause stress, or even anxiety, when it is not. This is particularly true when working with students suffering from issues such as trauma, anxiety, and depression.

Any well-sequenced class will minimize the risk of injury and anxiety. Teachers working with veterans should be particularly attentive to designing classes that maximally support the ability to learn to work with internal awareness (proprioception and interoception), relax deeply, and self-regulate, both physiologically and emotionally.

INSTRUCTIONAL BASICS 2: Teach Who's in the Room

Adapt class plans as necessary to meet student capabilities and needs.

A group yoga class may include students with a wide variety of physical abilities, as well as psychological and emotional states. To teach in a way that benefits all students, it is necessary to adapt the lesson plan and ongoing instruction to who is in the room. Teachers should consider age, physical strength, physical limitations, and any known psycho-emotional issues, and structure the class accordingly to maximize safety for each individual, while maintaining the energy and momentum of the group. To this effect, teachers should offer students a range of less to more challenging options for the same pose, and suggest additional modifications or alternate postures when necessary.

Experienced teachers working with veterans with PTSD should also be able to assess whether students would benefit from poses, breath work, and mindfulness exercises designed to counterbalance states of hyper- or hypo-arousal. For example, working with energizing, strength-demanding standing poses and ending with a shorter period of lying relaxation can help counterbalance hypo-arousal. Conversely, having more relaxing, supported seated postures and ending with a longer period of relaxation—perhaps lying on the floor with legs up the wall—can help counterbalance hyper-vigilance.[15]

INSTRUCTIONAL BASICS 3: Prioritize Breath Work

Teach students to work with their breath to help regulate the nervous system, and encourage them to take this skill "off the mat" into everyday life.

Working systematically with the breath to positively impact physiological and psycho-emotional health is an integral part of a mindful yoga practice. Teachers should start with simple breath instruction to balance the nervous system. Providing simple, scientifically grounded explanations of why this works physiologically can be helpful.[16]

Teachers should encourage students to maintain smooth, regulated breathing throughout class. They should remain alert, however, to signs that students are breathing in ways that carry unnecessary strain, or seem to be contributing to stress, rather than alleviating it. If a posture cannot be performed while maintaining a steady, even breath, this is generally a sign that students should back off on the intensity and/or that the teacher should downshift the pace.

Over time, teachers can help students explore what breath patterns help balance which states, and encourage them to consider practicing these tools in everyday life. For example, gradually developing the ability to match the length of long, slow, full inhales and exhales tends to be energizing. However, it is critical to

---

15 Lying on the back with legs up the wall, while generally experienced as calming to the nervous system, is not recommended for individuals with high blood pressure.

16 For a more detailed explanation of how yoga can help balance the nervous system, see the preceding sections on "Working with Trauma," especially Best Practices 1 and 2. The literature on trauma-informed yoga offers the best discussion of this critically important issue, which is relevant to all students, regardless of whether they have experienced trauma or not.

proceed with some caution when teaching regulated breathing. Instruction that inadvertently causes students to push too far, too fast could be dangerous, particularly for students with asthma, anxiety, or PTSD.

Similarly, certain breathing patterns could evoke military training exercises in disruptive and potentially triggering ways. For example, although doubling the length of the exhale to the inhale is often recommended for managing stress and reducing anxiety, some combat veterans have reported that they were trained to shoot in conjunction with a long, slow exhale. In this case, a breath exercise that is normally an important resource could alternatively be a trigger. One way to address this would be to teach a similar breathing pattern using a "sigh" out the mouth on exhale, as this is not the same as the focused exhale used for shooting.

INSTRUCTIONAL BASICS 4: Use Culturally Appropriate Language

Teach yoga using language that is sensitive to military culture, and conveys respect and support for veterans.

The careful use of language when teaching yoga is always important. When working with veterans, it is helpful to consider the use of language in light of general patterns of military training, culture, and experience.

Reorienting the "Mission." Members of the military have been trained to be "mission-oriented," follow a strict chain of command, and take action to complete the mission as directed, even in highly dangerous circumstances. In the context of a yoga class, they may perceive the teacher as the commander of the class and take any cues regarding poses as "orders" to follow. Veterans may push hard to achieve the given "mission," or pose, to the best of their ability, regardless of how they are feeling and what may be best for their bodies and psycho-emotional state.

Teachers should use language in ways that re-patterns this conditioning, encouraging veterans to tune into their physical condition and psycho-emotional state on a deeper level, and make choices concerning what variation of the pose (if any) is best for them to practice at any given moment. It is helpful to offer options throughout class so that participants do not reflexively "obey" the instructor, but start to develop an internal locus of control and sense how best to engage with their yoga practice from moment to moment.

Word choice. It is important for teachers to be aware of what words they are using and why. It is best to use positive cues to guide students in poses and give encouragement without coddling them. Examples of positively inflected cues include "consider," "work towards," "allow," "notice," "be curious," "approach with interest," "experiment," "when you are ready," and "if you like." Avoid negative and overly commanding words such as "don't," "must," "should," "never," "always," and "wrong."

Words used in specific military contexts, such as "surrender," "melt," "bind," "let go," or "corpse pose" may sound encouraging in a public yoga class, but they are not recommended for veterans. Instructors can use other words to describe how to get into a pose, or choose a more neutral name for a pose. For example, "corpse pose" (the standard translation for the traditional final resting pose of *Savasana)* can be referred to as "resting pose."

Be Concise. Postural cues work best when they are clear and concise. While teachers should be careful to avoid any sense that they are "barking orders," they should be equally mindful not to embellish their instruction with unnecessarily elaborate language.

During the course of instruction, it can be helpful to insert a few brief explanations of why and how particular poses may be beneficial (e.g., *"this type of breath work helps many people relax"*). Teachers should avoid making sweeping statements that might give students the sense that they "should" feel a particular way in a pose.

In general, yoga teachers should avoid making grandiose claims about yoga. Instead, they should offer basic, factual information about yoga as a means of empowering students with increased knowledge and understanding.

Setting an Intent. Some teachers may wish to invite students to "set an intent" for their practice at the beginning of class. This is a common feature of many classes, and typically involves prioritizing a particular physical movement (e.g., relaxing the jaw) or emotional attitude (e.g., practicing kindness toward one's self). If an invitation to set an intent is proffered, teachers should make sure to do it using language that is unambiguously secular. (See "Curriculum and Instruction I: General Guidelines," above.) In addition, it should be clearly communicated to students that setting an intent for their practice is entirely optional.

TEACHING AND CURRICULUM 4: TEACH SELF-REGULATION SKILLS

SELF-REGULATION 1: Teach Students to "Find Their Edge" Safely

Encourage veterans to "find their edge" safely by balancing force and ease.

Many veterans have internalized the well-known adage of "no pain, no gain." Often, they may want to push hard to "achieve" poses, or even become competitive with each other in performing more difficult ones. This behavior should be tactfully redirected. In addition to reinforcing—rather than re-patterning—the habit of prioritizing external goals rather than internal awareness, it can easily lead to injury.

Teachers can remind students that there is no end goal except their own self-awareness and personal health, which only they can fully determine. Teachers can encourage students to notice when they are developing stress in the body and/or mind as they hold a pose, and teach skills to help them release it. Teachers can also help veterans learn to titrate force with language that encourages them to *"come up to your edge of discomfort in this pose, and then back off to the point of no strain, or pain."*

Finding that "edge" can be a skill that takes time to learn. With ongoing reminders, refocusing, and reassurance, participants can learn to tolerate an appropriate level of discomfort, which enables them to engage with their yoga practice more deeply, while maintaining physical and psycho-emotional safety.

SELF-REGULATION 2: Develop Proprioception and Interoception

Teach yoga in ways that help develop greater internal awareness of the physical location of the body, as well as feelings and sensations within it.

The practice of yoga naturally increases proprioceptive skills (i.e., the ability to know where the body is in space through internal awareness). Teachers should consider how best to support students in developing proprioceptive awareness in friendly, curious, nonjudgmental ways. Clear, concise language that directs students to notice how their body feels—before and after a pose, on the right versus left side of the body, and so on—helps them build proprioceptive capacity. Helping students develop a set of sensory memories through repeating short sequences of synchronized movement and breath is also helpful.

Interoception is similar to proprioception in that both involve internal awareness. In this case, the focus is on feeling, sensation, and emotion, rather than physical movement and location. As Seppala (2012) explains, neuroscientists believe that engaging this internally focused state of awareness involves a different part of the brain than utilized by our more everyday, externally focused state. (Specifically, the former engages the "limbic bridge" areas, and the latter, the pre-frontal cortex.) Learning to work with these different parts of the brain has "important implications for emotional well-being," as it offers the opportunity to work with feelings directly, rather than having to process everything through concepts and language at all times.

Because military members have been trained to maintain tight emotional control, a yoga class that fosters relaxation and acknowledgement of personal feelings may be initially uncomfortable for them. It may be helpful to inform students that their experience of yoga may change from day to day, and even minute to minute. Class one day may feel great. The next day, the student might be tired, off balance, or challenged by sensations and feelings. Teachers can guide students to accept the different ways that they feel from day-to-day on the mat, and explain how this can translate to being able to meet the changing circumstances of life "off the mat" with increasing presence and ease. As much as possible, teachers should attune to students' psycho-emotional states and adjust their teaching to support them in exploring yoga at their own pace.

SELF-REGULATION 3: Facilitate Deep Relaxation

Make time for deep relaxation at the end of every class.

A period of deep relaxation is recommended for the end of every yoga session. It is important to give students a choice as to how they relax. Although the traditional relaxation posture practiced at the end of a yoga class, *Savasana,* involves lying on the back on the floor, this posture may cause some people to feel overly vulnerable. Yoga students who are better able to relax in some other position—lying on their stomachs, sitting in a chair, etc.—should be encouraged to do so.

Teachers should consider giving explicit permission to students to fall asleep during class or when doing similar exercises at home. While not a standard practice in civilian yoga classes, the opportunity to relax into sleep may be a priority for veterans, particularly if their nervous systems are hyper-aroused.

If students fall asleep in class and start snoring, simply direct other students to roll any sounds in the room into their relaxation. Also, if students know that they may fall asleep and that certain physical adjustments may alleviate snoring (e.g., elevating the torso), encourage them to make them prior to beginning the pose.

Teachers should consider using guided imagery or body scans to support a deep relaxation response. Imagery should be kept very general, as invoking specific settings (e.g., a beach or forest) may evoke disturbing memories. Body scans may include tensing and releasing different parts of the body, moving progressively from feet to crown.

Resting in silence for an extended period should be considered an advanced practice, and is not recommended for beginners. Long silences are particularly to be avoided for veterans with PTSD, as they may be discomforting or triggering.

SELF-REGULATION 4: Teach Self-Regulation for Empowerment

Teach veterans to utilize yoga-based skills as resources for self-regulation and personal empowerment in everyday life.

By developing a repertoire of yoga-based skills that includes not simply physical poses, but also breath work, proprioception, interoception, and relaxation, students gradually learn to regulate their own nervous systems, energy levels, and mental and emotional states more effectively. With time, the development of such self-regulatory skills enables people to experience a greater range of choices in everyday life. Rather than simply reacting to whatever thoughts and feelings come up in a given situation—or, conversely, forcibly overriding them to conform to a preset behavior—there is an enhanced ability to notice, process, and work with them intentionally.

Teachers may wish to gradually introduce students to the idea of self-regulation as a means of increasing one's capacity to make choices, and, consequently, a resource for personal empowerment.[17] As always, they will need to be working on deepening these skills in their own lives in order to teach them effectively to others.

---

17 For an excellent set of resources discussing self-regulation and related skills for empowerment through yoga and supporting practices written by a veteran for military personnel, veterans, and others see Plummer Taylor (2014, 2015).

BEST PRACTICES: GENDER CONSIDERATIONS

Given that approximately 90 percent of American veterans are men, most yoga classes for veterans will be predominantly male as well. Given that yoga tends to be more popular with women, the typical class is also likely to include them. Consequently, yoga teachers should be prepared to work in a predominantly male, but also mixed-gender environment. Also, since the repeal of the "Don't Ask, Don't Tell" policy in 2011 ended the prohibition of homosexuality in the military, making it safer for such personnel to be "out" regarding their sexual and gender identities, it is likely that classes will include veterans who self-identify as LBGTQ and/or are concerned about related issues.

Some yoga classes for service members and veterans are gender-specific: most commonly, women-only. Selected VAs have set up women-only classes as part of their treatment protocol for women suffering from Military Sexual Trauma (MST). Attendance at such therapeutic classes may be optional or mandated, depending on the program. (This set-up parallels VA classes designed to treat specific physical conditions, such as back pain.) In addition, yoga teachers working in studios, community organizations, or other settings serving veterans sometimes hold women-only classes to better serve that segment of the community.

Yoga teachers should be prepared to teach in ways that are maximally inclusive, supportive, and sensitive to every veteran they serve, regardless of gender and sexual identity. With this in mind, this section provides information and recommendations for yoga teachers and administrators seeking to set up programs and/or hire teachers.

GENDER CONSIDERATIONS 1: UNDERSTAND MILITARY CONTEXT

Yoga teachers should have a basic understanding of gender- and sexuality-related issues most relevant to veterans.

Issues of gender and sexuality have roiled the U.S. military in unprecedented ways since the 1990s. In many respects, this parallels developments in American society at large. Because the military has its own unique culture, structure, policies, and demands, however, no simple equivalence should be assumed. Core issues that need to be understood specifically in the context of the military include the changing status of women, policies surrounding sexual harassment and assault, and the rise and fall of the "Don't Ask, Don't Tell" (DADT) policy.

Back in the late 1990s, Dunivin (1997) argued that the process of integrating more equalitarian, inclusive values into the traditionally masculine, combat-ready, warrior-based culture of the U.S. military had produced internal divisions, particularly around issues of gender and sexuality. While "evolutionists" believed that women and homosexuals could and should be integrated into the military on an equalitarian basis, "traditionalists" saw this as neither feasible nor desirable.

Although much has changed since the 1990s, this analysis of the internal divisions produced by this ongoing "paradigm shift" in U.S. military culture remain relevant today. Yoga teachers should be ready to work with veterans who may express different views on these issues. They should also be prepared to do whatever is necessary to maintain a classroom environment that feels safe and welcoming to all.

Women Vets. Although women were not formally part of the military until the Army Nurse Corps was created in 1901, they have served informally since its inception. In 1973, the end of conscription and transition to the All-Volunteer

Force dramatically increased women's opportunities to serve (NCVAS, 2011). By 2015, women accounted for 20 percent of new recruits, 14.5 percent of the 1.4 million active duty force, and 18 percent of the 850,000 reserve force (Petersen, 2015). Women also account for 1.6 million of the nation's 20.2 million veterans (U.S. Census, 2015).

An unprecedented number of women served in the Iraq (OIF) and Afghanistan (OEF) conflicts—approximately 300,000 since September 11, 2001 (Tilghman, 2015). These wars drastically changed the role of women in the military by placing them in the same everyday danger as their male counterparts. Although formally barred from combat until January 2016, in practice, no meaningful "front line" has existed to divide combat and non-combat positions in these conflicts. At the same time, women have been serving in positions traditionally held by men, such as gunners in convoys sitting in the turrets of military vehicles behind machine guns (Halvorson, 2010).

A recent study, however, found only 37 percent of women veterans feel "recognized, respected and valued as veterans in civilian life." Many feel "isolated, unacknowledged and invisible" in a society that either cannot fathom what they've experienced, or discounts their military experience as "somehow less challenging" than that of men (Petersen, 2015). Even among fellow vets, many women feel their status is erased. For example, when a woman vet attends a veterans' event with her civilian husband, it is commonly assumed that he is the veteran, and she is not.

This lack of recognition has a negative impact. Even in the military, women's status as a gender minority reduces opportunities to develop social bonds and camaraderie. High rates of sexual harassment and abuse make this already challenging situation worse. Because social support is a known factor that increases resilience, any sense of social isolation that develops for female service members makes whatever challenges arise during their military experience more difficult to navigate.

Many women find returning to civilian life especially difficult due to the lack of understanding of their experience, and the challenge of tapping into a strong network of social support. The resultant sense of isolation can be devastating. In 2014, almost 4,500 of the nation's 58,000 homeless vets are women. Further, half of this number reported sexual harassment or abuse during their service (Banks, 2014). Suicide rates for women rise sharply upon leaving the military, and occur at an "obscenely high" rate that is six times that of their civilian counterparts (Zarembo, 2015).

This is not to suggest that all women in the military experience these problems, or that their experience is always more challenging than that of men. As noted above, yoga teachers (and others) should never make assumptions about veterans' experiences, and women vets are no exception. That said, it is important to be aware of these issues, should they arise, in order to be better prepared to support students.

LGBTQ Veterans. Officially, the U.S. military defined itself in opposition to homosexuality after World War I with the 1917 Articles of War, which outlawed sodomy. In practice, the military has a record of retaining gays and lesbians during times of war, only to discharge them during peacetime (Bateman, 2004).

Until the passage of DADT in 1993, service members who were found to have engaged in homosexual conduct were likely to receive discharges designated "Less than Honorable." A dishonorable discharge can have severe consequences that follow veterans the rest of their lives. In most states, it is legal for private employers to discriminate on the basis of discharge characterization. Further, a Less than Honorable discharge all but disqualifies a person from working in the public sector. It may also mean forfeiture of veterans' benefits, such as G.I. Bill education benefits, and health care coverage (Miller and Cray, 2013).

Forged as a compromise between military traditionalists and evolutionists during the Clinton Administration, DADT was in force during 1993-2011. DADT held that gays and lesbians could remain in the military as long as they did not openly declare their sexual orientation. Most service members who were discharged for "homosexual conduct" under DADT received Honorable or General Under Honorable discharges. While not as severe as a Less than Honorable discharge, DADT "nevertheless exacted a serious toll on the careers" of the over 14,000 gay and lesbian military personnel discharged under it (Bateman, 2004; Miller and Cray, 2013).[18]

In 2011, the Obama Administration rescinded DADT. In 2013, the Supreme Court struck down Section 3 of the Defense of Marriage Act (DOMA), which denied over 1,000 federal benefits and protections available to heterosexual couples to married same-sex couples. Consequently, sexual orientation is no longer grounds for dismissal from the military, and the federal government—including the DOD—now recognizes same-sex spouses for the purpose of federal benefits. However, it remains unclear whether gay and lesbian veterans will receive spousal benefits if they do not reside in a state that recognizes same-sex marriage. Further, some veterans who were discharged for being gay or lesbian are still fighting for a discharge upgrade, which affects their ability to gain health care coverage and find employment (Miller and Cray, 2013).

Transgender Veterans. The U.S. Department of Defense implemented a new policy allowing transgender people to serve openly throughout the military services in July 2016. This policy also requires the Pentagon to cover the medical costs of service members seeking to undergo gender transition. New recruits who are transgender are required to spend at least 18 months in their transitioned gender identity before joining the military.

A recent RAND Corporation study commissioned by the Secretary of Defense estimated that of 1.3 million active-duty service members, approximately 2,450 are transgender, and that an additional 65 may seek to make a gender transition annually (Rosenberg, 2016). Given that transgender people were not allowed to serve openly in the military prior to mid-2016, the number of transgender veterans is unknown.

18 DADT disproportionately impacted women: During the seven years in which was in effect, women comprised 13.6% of the military, but were 25.9% of the relevant discharges.

Military Sexual Trauma (MST). The VA defines MST as "psychological trauma, which in the judgment of a mental health professional employed by the Department, resulted from a physical assault of a sexual nature, battery of a sexual nature, or sexual harassment which occurred while the Veteran was serving on active duty or active duty for training."[19] By law, VAs must screen all patients for MST, and provide treatment for it. Of those screened, 15-36 percent of women and 1-2 percent of men were assessed as having MST (Stander and Thomsen, 2016).

A lower reported MST prevalence rate among male veterans should not be taken to mean that men's MST is not a problem. On the contrary, the actual numbers of male versus female MST cases identified by the VA are quite similar. In 2005, for example, universal screening identified 6,227 cases of men's MST and 6,469 cases of women's MST. Further, these data do not represent the full scope of male or female MST, as they are limited to screened veterans and based on self-reports (Hoyt et al, 2011).

The DOD began assessing rates of sexual harassment and assault in the military in 1988. Recent DOD data indicate that although reporting rates of sexual assault increased dramatically during 2004-2014 (rising from 1,700 to 6,131 reported incidents), only 25% of service members who experienced unwanted sexual contact actually reported it to a military authority. A 2015 RAND study found that found that about 1% of male and 5% of female active duty service members experienced a sexual assault; approximately 7% of these men and 22% of the women experienced sexual harassment. Data on veterans shows about 1 in 4 women and 1 in 100 men report having experienced MST (afterdeployment.org, 2015).

Considerable research has focused on the impact of sexual victimization while in the military, primarily for female service members. Evidence shows that long-term effects can be serious and wide-ranging, including physical (e.g.,

---

19 The DOD, in contrast, defines and responds to sexual harassment and assault separately, in line with distinctions made in the military and civilian criminal justice systems.

chronic health problems, pain, obesity), mental (PTSD, depression), and behavioral (substance abuse, eating disorders, employment difficulties, relationship problems) issues. Although not as many studies have examined the impact of sexual trauma on military men, the consequences appear to be at least equally severe (Hoyt et al, 2011).

Current evidence suggests that the impacts of sexual harassment and assault are similar. For those who have experienced multiple incidents involving both of these types of sexual victimization, more severe cumulative effects are likely. Military stressors such as combat exposure may exacerbate them further. Research indicates that the negative impact of sexual harassment and assault may be even greater for service members than for civilian victims, particularly if they are forced to continue working with their perpetrator, or feel a profound sense of betrayal after an assault by a fellow service member (ibid.).

GENDER CONSIDERATIONS 2: DON'T MAKE ASSUMPTIONS

Do not make assumptions about sexual harassment or abuse, MST, or other military or personal experiences based on a veteran's gender or sexual identity.

While it is important to be informed about issues of gender and sexual identity, it is equally important to not make assumptions concerning veterans' personal experiences. For example, civilian yoga teachers should not automatically envision women veterans as victims of an all-male environment. Nor should it be assumed that they suffer from MST, or that they were otherwise traumatized by their military experience.

It is similarly important not to characterize MST as a "women's issue." Although MST is certainly an issue of tremendous concern to women vets, it is a problem that impacts everyone. As noted above, although research indicates significantly higher reported prevalence and incidence rates in women than men, the actual number of cases identified by the VA is very similar (ibid.).[20]

GENDER CONSIDERATIONS 3: CONSIDER WOMEN-ONLY CLASSES

Consider offering yoga classes and/or workshops specifically for women veterans as a means of facilitating social connections and supporting women's health.

Offering women-only yoga classes or workshops can be an important way to connect women vets with one another and support gender-specific health concerns (e.g., pregnancy). Social isolation is common among women veterans, and greater social support increases resilience and supports mental health. This, in turn, reduces stress and improves physical health. In this sense, facilitating social connections and supporting women's health are highly complementary goals.

Specific points to keep in mind for teachers interested in developing women-only classes and workshops for veterans, as well as active-duty service members, include the following:

- Consider offering specialized workshops on women's health issues in settings that have a high number of female military personnel and/or family members (e.g., large bases).
- Every VA Medical Center employs a Women Veterans Program Manager (WVMP) to assist women veterans and coordinate services for them. Yoga teachers interested in setting up women-only classes at VAMCs should seek out the local WVMP and seek to enlist their support.

---

20 Given that gay, lesbian, and bisexual military personnel were required to conceal their sexual identify prior to the repeal of DADT, and that transgender individuals had to do so until July 2016, there is no comparable data on LGBTQ vets. In one of the few relevant studies available, Cochran et al (2013) found that rates of depression, PTSD, and alcohol use were higher for LGB veterans utilizing VA services than their heterosexual counterparts. These LGB veterans also reported high rates of suicidal thoughts and behavior, with almost 15% having made a serious suicide attempt.

- Ensure that teachers leading classes for women with targeted health issues have received the appropriate specialized training (e.g., certification in prenatal yoga, teaching yoga and meditation to survivors of MST).
- Structure classes for women veterans in VAs, community organizations, yoga studios, and other settings in ways that facilitate connections among them. A great way to do this is to schedule in at least 10 minutes after class ends for informal socializing. This allows a sense of community to grow organically by providing time and space for conversation and socializing.
- If a women-only class is being held in a VA, be aware that everyone will need to exit the room punctually. So, if a room is allotted for an hour, teach a 45-minute class, and reserve 15 minutes after it ends for informal socializing.
- Recognize that while women vets have much in common, they are also a diverse group. If appropriate, seek to learn more about whatever subgroups may be present in class (e.g., racial or sexual minorities). When possible, a good way to do this is by identifying a knowledgeable informal leader for the group. For example, if there is an established group of African American women veterans, and many of them are coming to yoga, connect with the organizer of the group to discuss how you might serve them better.
- Welcome transgender women veterans into non-clinical women-only classes if that is their preference. (Whether this might be overly disruptive in therapeutic classes, particularly those for women suffering from MST, should be assessed on a case-by-case basis.)

GENDER CONSIDERATIONS 4: CONSIDER TEACHER-STUDENT DYNAMICS

Consider how gender may impact the teacher-student relationship, both in mixed-gender and gender-specific classes.

Program administrators charged with hiring yoga teachers, as well as yoga teachers themselves, should consider how gender dynamics may affect the teacher-student relationship, and impact military personnel in the class. As noted above, military demographics dictate that the typical yoga class will be mixed gender, but predominantly male. This is not always the case: Settings such as VFWs and community organizations may have a preponderance of women.

Female teachers working with predominantly male groups must be comfortable in this environment, and not easily rattled by the occasional off-color joke. By the same token, they must have the maturity to minimize whatever sexual energies their presence may spark. Given these capacities, there is no reason that a woman can't successfully teach yoga to classes predominantly composed of men.

Conversely, men teaching a predominantly male class that is also mixed-gender must be committed to maintaining environment that feels welcoming to women, and have the awareness and maturity necessary to do so. In such cases, male teachers can provide an excellent role model for male and female students alike, who can benefit from seeing a male leader in a role that tends to be associated with women.

If a class is mixed-gender but has a majority of women, having either a male or female teacher is fine. If a class is explicitly restricted to women, it is strongly recommended that the teacher be female as well. This gender matching represents standard practice in the field in general.

Some women veterans have a strong preference for having a female vet teach a women-only class if possible. In their view, having a woman vet as a teacher provides a form of positive role modeling that an equally qualified civilian teacher cannot. Other women veterans have no such preference and feel as strongly that a civilian teacher with the requisite training and experience can be as effective. All agree that the first concern should be to hire an appropriately qualified teacher.

RELATIONSHIP BUILDING BEST PRACTICES

Positive, supportive relationships are essential to human health and well-being. Although yoga is in many ways a highly individualized pursuit—adaptable to different personal needs, and facilitative of self-inquiry and self-awareness—it is most effective when practiced in a context that values and supports healthy interpersonal relationships. This section discusses Best Practices for a variety of relationships relevant to teaching yoga to veterans, ranging from self-care to professional networks, and beyond.

RELATIONSHIP BUILDING 1: PRACTICE SELF-CARE

Yoga teachers should commit to practicing self-care as a means of supporting themselves and others.

While it is important for everyone to practice self-care, it is particularly vital for yoga teachers and others in the helping professions. When substantial time and energy is devoted to supporting others, it's critical to devote time to "recharging your batteries." If this doesn't happen, it will likely have a negative impact not only on the teachers, but also on their ability to teach and support students.

Yoga teachers should be aware that what's required for effective self-care may change in response to fluctuating demands on their time and energy. Remaining aware of what's truly needed, and making time for that, is a constant, often challenging one. Teachers who recognize and respect their own needs for self-care will be happier and healthier, as well as better able to teach well and handle challenges with insight and grace.

It is important to realize that in some cases, practicing effective self-care may require engaging outside supports. This may include requesting assistance from a family member or close friend, or engaging professional help from a physical or psychological therapist. Yoga teachers should seek to embody and model a willingness and ability to seek and accept appropriate supports from others as an ongoing part of their teaching and personal practice.

RELATIONSHIP BUILDING 2: MAINTAIN HEALTHY TEACHER-STUDENT RELATIONSHIPS

Understand the psychology of the teacher-student relationship, and how to maintain it within safe, supportive, healthy boundaries.

Yoga teachers should have the training and maturity necessary to recognize any tendencies on the part of students to idealize or unconsciously project feelings onto them. Such psychological transference is very common in the yoga world, although it is not recognized as such as much as it should be. All yoga teachers should be aware of these dynamics. This is particularly critical for those working with groups in which there may be a higher than average incidence of trauma.

Having students experience emotional projections onto their teacher is not necessarily a negative thing. Often, it is simply a normal part of the process that many people undergo as they learn to work with yoga as a mind-body integration practice, as opposed to simply stretching and exercise. This may arise when formerly repressed feelings are activated in ways that cause some of them to be unconsciously projected onto the teacher.

In such cases, teachers must have the skills necessary to "hold the space" and provide students with the opportunity to work through whatever comes up for them in their practice at their own pace. Teachers must have the personal maturity to remain unprovoked by student projections, needing neither to affirm those that feed their

egos, nor shut down those that spark their insecurities.

As noted in the "Curriculum and Instruction" section, yoga teachers should maintain strict professional boundaries. They must remember they are not therapists (either physical or mental health) and be ready to refer students to appropriate therapeutic supports as needed. Teachers should not share overly personal or contact information, and avoid any words or actions that could unintentionally carry sexual connotations. They should also clearly communicate whether and how they are available to speak with students outside of class, and honor their word to the letter.

RELATIONSHIP BUILDING 3: BUILD TRUST AND TEAMWORK

Leverage military values that emphasize trust and teamwork to facilitate the development of supportive yoga communities and long-lasting connections.

One of the advantages of teaching yoga classes for veterans is that military personnel appreciate group dynamics. Given common values and socialization, once veterans form relationships with other veterans, a strong bond of trust tends to develop. Yoga teachers should be aware of these special dynamics, and support the development of a robust team spirit, rooted in trust.

If new students join an ongoing class, teachers should consider giving more seasoned students an opportunity to welcome them, and perhaps say a few words about how they've found the class helpful.

RELATIONSHIP BUILDING 4: SOLICIT STUDENT FEEDBACK

Solicit student feedback about their experience in class and with yoga more generally by means of anonymous surveys on a regular basis.

Giving regular, anonymous surveys to solicit student feedback on their experience in class, and with yoga overall, can be a vital tool for facilitating open teacher-student communications and improving instructional and program quality. Such open feedback loops help to build student trust by giving them the opportunity to express their thoughts and feelings in a safe, supported way. Students are empowered when they see their input is encouraged and valued. This makes it clear that learning can be a two-way street, involving both teacher and student.

Programs located in VAs should consider structuring such surveys into their larger program evaluation protocol (see "Best Practices for Teaching in the VA," below). Likewise, other programs could use student surveys as the basis for simple self-evaluations. Survey-generated data is also valuable to have when applying for grants or seeking other sources of funding.

RELATIONSHIP BUILDING 5: HAVE TEACHER SUPPORT SYSTEMS

Yoga teachers should develop relationships with peers, mental health professionals, physical therapists, caregivers, and others as needed to support themselves and their students.

Yoga teachers may be called on to teach in challenging circumstances, particularly within the VA and other clinical settings. It is crucial that they have support systems in place to help themselves and their students when problems and questions arise. Key connections to consider include:

- *Peer Support.* Yoga teachers serving veterans have a unique skill set and experience that other yoga teachers cannot fully replicate. Having connections with trusted and respected peers they can turn to for support and guidance as necessary is an invaluable resource.
- *Military Professionals.* Teachers working in the VA, DOD, or other military settings should have a contact person who they can reach out to if they detect real or potential issues with students (e.g., evidence of problems with medication, unusual emotional volatility, inappropriate conduct).
- *Mental Health Professionals.* It is very important that teachers working in VAs or other clinical settings have a relationship with a clinician who understands the yoga program, and can offer guidance and support as needed. In some cases, it is ideal to have a mental health professional physically in the room during classes. Clinicians assigned to a yoga class typically observe and take notes that go into participants' files.
- *Physical and Recreational* Th*erapists.* These professionals may similarly be in the VA classroom when yoga is taught to veterans with severe physical injuries. In this case, yoga teachers should develop a working relationship with them that best supports the needs of each individual student.
- *Caregivers.* Veterans with severe injuries studying yoga outside of a VA may come to class with a caregiver. In such cases, it is crucial to connect with the caregiver and discuss how to support students safely.

RELATIONSHIP BUILDING 6: FACILITATE VETERAN-CIVILIAN CONNECTIONS

Seek opportunities to facilitate positive connections between veterans and civilians.

In keeping with the widely acknowledged divergence between military and civilian culture that has developed in the post-Vietnam era, many veterans report feeling disconnected and alienated from civilian life after completing their service. A 2009 study to identify risk factors for suicide interviewed returned combat veterans and found that many experienced "a loss of sense of self and purpose post-discharge":

Many veterans found it difficult to leave their well-defined and meaningful military roles to reestablish their place in the civilian world. Veterans also reported a heightened sense of burdensomeness and described struggling to provide their families with financial and emotional support. Many also reported feeling disconnected from civilians. This was in contrast to the sense of belongingness they felt when among those in the military or other veterans. During the course of the interviews, veterans linked perceived burdensomeness and a failed sense of belongingness with a desire for death (Brenner and Barnes, 2012).

Given yoga's ubiquity in civilian life and growing popularity among veterans, classes held in non-military settings (e.g., studios and community organizations) can potentially facilitate positive veteran-civilian connections. Of course, events would have to be designed thoughtfully to minimize the risk of producing unintentionally alienating encounters. If set up by knowledgeable teachers with strong ties in both communities, however, it should be possible to facilitate positive connections capable of enriching the lives of veterans and civilians alike.

BEST PRACTICES FOR THE VA

The VA is comprised of three administrations: The Veterans Health Administration (VHA), Veterans Benefits Administration (VBA), and National Cemetery Administration (NCA). The VHA is the largest administration within the VA, and comprises America's largest integrated health care system. (Following common usage, this book refers to the VHA simply as "the VA." Because the VBA and NCA are not pertinent to the issue of yoga for veterans, they are not included in this discussion.) Currently, the VHA encompasses over 1,700 sites of care including hospitals, community based outpatient clinics, nursing homes, domiciliaries, and 300 Vet Centers. This system serves 8.76 million veterans annually. It employs over 300,000 health care professionals and support staff at the various sites of care, 80,000 of whom are veterans themselves.

The VA's mission is to honor America's veterans by providing exceptional health care that improves their health and well-being. Services provided within the VA are broad and include primary care, mental health care, and specialty care services. Within each of these categories, the VA provides both standard health care services and specialized offerings uniquely tailored to veterans. Examples of vital VA offerings include amputation care, blind rehabilitation services, environmental exposure care, military sexual trauma (MST) counseling, polytrauma/traumatic brain injury care, post-deployment health care, post-traumatic stress disorder (PTSD) care, prosthetic and sensory aid services, readjustment counseling, spinal cord injury care, and substance abuse care.

Currently, the VA is working to shift its culture of health care provision from one rooted in problem-based "sick care" to one dedicated to "Whole Health" care, which will engage and inspire veterans to attain their highest level of health and well-being. The Whole Health model integrates physical and psychosocial care with an individualized consideration of a veteran's personal health and goals. Developed to provide personalized, proactive, patient-driven care through multidisciplinary teams of health professionals, including some integrative health professionals, this approach includes complementary and integrative health (CIH) services such as acupuncture, massage, and mind-body techniques including, but not limited to yoga (Shulkin, 2016).

A study conducted by the VA in 2011 found that 89 percent of 141 surveyed VA medical facilities either offered CIH services or referred patients to external practitioners (VA 2011; Pence, 2014).[21] Of the ten CIH modalities surveyed, meditation was the most commonly provided. Yoga was ninth, with 44 of the 141 facilities providing yoga services. The top five reported reasons for providing CIH services were promoting wellness, patient preference, as an adjunct to chronic care, proven clinical effect, and provider request. These findings, combined with the overall commitment of the VA to Whole Health care and countless positive reports from the field, suggest that there is tremendous potential for yoga offerings to grow in the VA at this time.[22]

BEST PRACTICES FOR THE VA 1: DEVELOPING A PROGRAM

DEVELOPING A PROGRAM 1: Understand Organizational Structure

Yoga teachers should understand the basic structure of the VA.

---

21 This study followed the once standard, but now outmoded practice of referring to CIH services as CAM, or "complementary and alternative medicine." The term "CIH" is used here instead because it is now the recommended terminology.

22 For additional information on CIH-related research in the VA, see http://www.research.va.gov/topics/cam.cfm.

Historically, the VHA system has been variable and decentralized. A well-known insider adage is: "*When you've seen one VA, you've seen one VA.*"[23] Consequently, while it's important to be familiar with the core set of organizational structures that operate under the broad umbrella of the VA, understanding the particular options in any given locality requires direct investigation. Key types of facilities include:

- *VA Medical Centers (VAMCs):* In addition to traditional hospital services, most of these Centers offer medical and surgical specialty services such as audiology and speech pathology, dermatology, dental, geriatrics, neurology, oncology, podiatry, prosthetics, urology, and vision care. While providing care to veterans, the VA also enables 100,000 medical professionals a year to receive required practicum training and conduct research across a wide spectrum of the medical field. Some of the existing 150 VMAC sites are integrated with local universities.[24]

- *Community-Based Outpatient Clinics (CBOCs):* These satellite clinics provide the most common outpatient services, including primary care and health and wellness visits, to patients who may have difficulty visiting a larger medical center because of distance or time. The VA has been expanding the network of CBOCs to include more rural locations, putting access to care closer to home. There are currently over 800 CBOCs.

- *Community Living Centers (CLCs):* CLCs are skilled nursing facilities, often referred to as "nursing homes." These facilities serve veterans

---

23 Since 2014, the VA has been pursuing the largest restructuring in its history under the "MyVA" initiative. Intended to improve access, quality, and efficiency across the system, this process is anticipated to be ongoing for many years (Daly 2014, VA 2015). For more information on the history and structure of the VA, visit the VA website, http://www.va.gov/landing2_about.htm.

24 The VA is America's largest provider of graduate medical education and a major contributor to medical and scientific research. More than 76,000 active volunteers, 118,000 health profession trainees, and 25,000 affiliated medical faculty are an integral part of the VH community. Roughly 60 percent of all medical residents obtain a portion of their training at VA hospitals.

with chronic stable conditions such as dementia, those requiring rehabilitation, or those who need comfort and care at the end of life. There are currently 135 CLCs.

- *Domiciliaries:* These are temporary residential units open to ambulatory veterans who do not need hospitalization or nursing home care, but do need rehabilitation and extensive medical support. In most communities, there is a focus on those who have slipped into homelessness.[25] This secure, homelike environment provides a wide range of medical, and/or psychiatric care, as well as vocational and educational counseling.

- *Vet Centers:* Vet Centers provide readjustment counseling and outreach services to veterans in community settings that are easily accessible to them and their families, yet separate from VA organizational sites to ensure confidential counseling and reduce barriers to care. All Vet Center services are prepaid through military service. Services are also available for family members dealing with military-related issues. The VA operates 300 community-based Vet Centers in all 50 states, as well the District of Columbia, Guam, Puerto Rico, and the U.S. Virgin Islands.

Contracting with Yoga Teachers. As discussed in the "Staffing and Training Best Practices" section, yoga is an unregulated field that lacks an authoritative credentialing system. This is true both within the field in general, and the VA in particular. There is no official "yoga teacher" job classification within the Federal Government's Office of Personnel Management (OPM). This situation necessarily generates a good deal of variation and challenges with regard to the terms under which yoga teachers are contracted to work in the VA and other federal agencies.

---

25 There are also VA-wide initiatives working towards ending homelessness among veterans. For more information, see http://www.va.gov/homeless/.

Within the VA, yoga teachers may work under various auspices, including but not limited to Voluntary Services,[26] Work without Compensation (WOC), external contracts, and grant-funded projects. In some cases, VA staff employed in some other capacity (e.g., recreational therapists) who also have yoga teacher certification may be approved to provide classes under the scope of their existing job classification.

The Integrative Health Coordinating Center (IHCC) within the VA's Office of Patient Centered Care and Cultural Transformation was formed to assist with identifying and addressing barriers to providing complementary and integrative health (CIH) services, including but not limited to yoga, across the VA system. IHCC staff are currently exploring how best to improve implementation of yoga and other complementary and integrative health services.

DUNS number. Yoga teachers should be aware that a Data Universal Numbering System (DUNS) number is required to contract with many Federal Government Agencies, including the VA.[27] This requirement applies to both individuals and organizations. Getting a DUNS number can be a lengthy and challenging process. Trainings are available, however, to help navigate it. Teachers who are contracting with VA or other organizations should work with their designated Point of Contact (POC) within the VA for guidance.

DEVELOPING A PROGRAM 2: Research Local Facilities

Yoga teachers seeking to offer services through the VA should become well acquainted with the various facilities offered in their geographic area.

As evidenced by the above list, there will be a number of different types of facilities to explore. Yoga teachers seeking to offer services through the VA should be aware that each facility has a slightly different mission focus and administrative

---

26 Information on VA Voluntary Services can be found on the VA website at http://www.volunteer.va.gov.

27 A DUNS fact sheet is available for free download via the VA website at http://www.va.gov/osdbu/docs/factsheetDUNS.pdf.

structure. Learning these particularities will likely be important to program set-up, development, and sustainability. Locations of all facilities can be found on the VA website.[28]

In addition to these federal facilities, each state has at least one state Veterans Home. These facilities provide nursing home, domiciliary, or adult day care and are owned, operated, and managed by state governments. (The VA does not manage state Veterans Homes.) Reports from the field suggest that these facilities tend to be very receptive to yoga programs.[29]

DEVELOPING A PROGRAM 3:
Research Current VA Priorities and Initiatives

Develop a basic understanding of current VA priorities and strategic initiatives by talking to knowledge sources and/or conducting web-based and other research.

If possible, yoga teachers and others seeking to set up yoga programs in the VA should have an up-to-date understanding of basic VA priorities and strategic initiatives. It is particularly important to have this baseline knowledge before making any sort of formal presentation to VA staff.

As a government entity, the VA is sensitive to the political climate, and may need to shift its prioritizes as it changes. Understanding current priorities for the VA, and being able to explain how yoga services can help meet those needs, should make it easier for a facility to support the development of proposed yoga programming.

In most cases, asking knowledgeable insiders for a briefing on current VA priorities and strategic initiatives will be the best way to obtain this information.

---

28 See the "Locations" page of the VA website, http://www.va.gov/landing2_locations.htm.

29 General information on state veterans homes is available in the "Geriatrics and Extended Care Page" section of the VA website; see http://www.va.gov/GERIATRICS/Guide/LongTermCare/State_Veterans_Homes.asp.

If insider contacts are not available, the best strategy may be to research this on the Internet, and then inquire about it again as new contacts are made.

DEVELOPING A PROGRAM 4: Seek an "Internal Champion"

Network through individuals, departments, and organizations to find a strong advocate for developing a yoga program within your local VA.

For yoga teachers seeking to set up programs in the VA, getting that first "foot in the door" can be challenging. Given the many different types of VA facilities, as well as the variation within each type, there are many different ways to do so. No single approach is universally successful.

Often, the easiest way to start the process of developing a yoga program is to find, or be introduced to an "internal champion": that is, a staff member who is dedicated, enthusiastic, and able to open doors. Other possibilities include contacting the leadership of a facility (e.g., the Director, Chief of Staff, and/or Nurse Executive), and scheduling a visit that can include a short presentation. Other successful avenues may include networking through contacts at women's clinics, integrative health centers, resident substance abuse programs, mental health services, chaplain services, physical or recreational therapy departments, and adaptive sports in VA medical centers.

Eventually, it is ideal to have a strong supporter within the VA who works at the executive or service chief level (e.g., a medical director or chief of voluntary services). People working at this level generally have the requisite knowledge and clout to maximize support for the program. Many VA medical centers also have Health Promotion Disease Prevention (HPDP) and/or Patient Centered Care (PCC) Coordinators. Similarly dedicated to a proactive, personalized, and integrative health and wellness models, both the HPDP and PCC are promising fits for yoga programs.[30]

---

30 For more information, see the VA's National Center for Health Promotion and Disease Prevention and Office of Patient Centered Care and Cultural Transformation websites; http://www.prevention.va.gov and http://www.va.gov/patientcenteredcare/.

DEVELOPING A PROGRAM 5: Demonstrate Professionalism

Understand, respect, and adapt as necessary to work smoothly within the conservative, yet diverse and eclectic culture of the VA.

All interactions with the VA should be conducted in a professional, businesslike manner. Wear business casual clothing. Avoid jewelry or badges on clothing, cars, or other personal items that make political or religious statements. Jeans are not appropriate. Yoga clothes should be strictly reserved for teaching, and more modest than is the norm in civilian gyms and studios.

Yoga teachers should be easily able to find many open-minded individuals working within the VA, including many who are interested in integrative health. In fact, many VAs employ people with extensive expertise in, and dedication to integrative health care, and many facilities offer strong integrative health services. What is possible and acceptable in terms of yoga services will, however, vary substantially among different programs and locations in accordance with local cultural norms, and relevant regional policies and priorities.

DEVELOPING A PROGRAM 6: Explain the Benefits of Yoga

Yoga teachers should be prepared to explain the benefits of yoga in a scientific, medically relevant, concise, and accessible way.

Before reaching out to the VA, yoga teachers should be confident that they are ready to communicate the benefits of yoga for veterans in a scientific, medically relevant, concise, and accessible way. They should also consider how to tailor information for different audiences and situations. For example, when speaking with directors, health care providers, and others in leadership positions, it may be appropriate to use more specialized terminology and provide a greater level of detail than might otherwise be appropriate (e.g., explaining how specific asanas (postures) and sequences can alleviate particular conditions such as low back pain or hypertension, or reduce hyper-vigilance).

Yoga teachers should understand that evidence-based practice is a priority for the VA, and have a basic understanding of current scientific literature regarding the benefits and risks of yoga in health care settings. One important report to be aware of is the "Evidence Map of Yoga for High-Impact Conditions Affecting Veterans" published by the VA's Health Services Research and Development Service in 2014.[31] This study concluded that the existing research literature provided strong evidence that yoga could help chronic low back pain, and suggestive evidence that it could help alleviate anxiety, depression, insomnia, and pain (Coeytaux, 2014).[32]

Yoga teachers should additionally consider the following communication aids:

- *"Elevator Speech."* Yoga teachers should be prepared to deliver an impromptu "elevator speech" that succinctly pitches what they can offer and explains why it's important to the VA. Connecting with someone who may prove key to setting up a successful program could happen at any moment.
- *One-Page Flyer.* Consider developing a one-page flyer that highlights your program offerings and includes your contact information and relevant credentials. Have this ready to hand out at any time. (Note: Offering flyers to veterans in a VA medical facility would most likely require an internal vetting process for approval prior to distribution.)
- *Mini-Presentation.* Develop a 10- to 15-minute presentation on the benefits of yoga for veterans. Ideally, this should include a reference to the "Evidence Map of Yoga for High-Impact Conditions Affecting Veterans" (ibid.), as well as strategic goals and priorities for yoga services for veterans within the VA. When discussing the possibility of a yoga program with administrators and other staff, let them know that this presentation is available to share with them at a convenient time, free of charge.

---

31 Both a full and summary versions of this report are available as free PDF downloads online at http://www.hsrd.research.va.gov/publications/esp/yoga.cfm.

32 For an important compilation of cutting-edge neuroscience research on yoga and other "movement-based embodied contemplative practices," see Schmalzl and Kerr, 2016.

DEVELOPING A PROGRAM 7: Consider a Pilot Program

Yoga teachers seeking to establish a new program in the VA should consider developing a small pilot program that they are willing to offer free of charge.

As noted in the "Staffing and Training Best Practices" section, once a yoga program is established, it may be preferable to staff it with paid teachers, rather than volunteers. When initially seeking to develop a program, however, teachers should consider offering a short pilot program (e.g., 6 to 12 sessions) for free.[33]

The pilot program should be designed to showcase the lead teacher's expertise, and the benefits of what they have to offer. Both staff and veterans should be invited to participate. In many cases, staff are the most willing to try classes when they are first offered. Often, they quickly become enthusiastic students, and key supporters of a program.

DEVELOPING A PROGRAM 8: Consider a Program for Staff

Consider developing a yoga program dedicated to serving VA staff.

A dedicated yoga program for VA staff can make a vital contribution to the organization, while supporting the VA's commitment to employee engagement. In particular, yoga can help address and manage employee stress and burnout. Reports from the field indicate that such programs are often welcome and appreciated.

Yoga teachers should be aware that staff may need to attend yoga classes on off-duty hours or during breaks. The best timing for classes would need to be decided by the facility's leadership, likely through their Occupational Health program. Again, a good way to explore the possibility of setting up such a program

---

33 For free resources designed to assist with the development of pilot programs in the VA, including an program evaluation protocol developed at the Salt Lake VA (Utah), see Green Tree Yoga, "How to Start a Program," http://www.greentreeyoga.org/veterans-how-to-start-a-program.

would be propose a pilot. Generally, this would also be set up through Occupational Health.

BEST PRACTICES FOR THE VA 2: TEACHING IN THE VA

TEACHING IN THE VA 1: Work with Available Space

Yoga teachers should clearly communicate their needs regarding classroom and prop storage space, while remaining ready to work within the constraints of available space.

It is prudent to expect and plan for logistical challenges when attempting to teach classes in any nontraditional setting, including the VA. Space is at a premium in most hospital settings. Healthcare buildings and clinics were never designed to house yoga classes. Rooms may be small and cramped. The space available may not be ideal in terms of temperature settings, lighting, or ambient noise. Room assignments may frequently and unexpectedly change.

Yoga teachers should work with their point of contact and hospital administrators to help them understand the role of props and the need for secure storage place between classes. Yoga teachers are responsible for explaining what's needed and why, working with staff to identify the best option available, and complying with hospital policies and procedures.

When establishing a program, teachers should have a clear sense of their ideal class size, and corresponding type and number of props. They should also cap the maximum acceptable number of students. Resultant classroom and prop storage space needs should be clearly communicated to their POC and relevant staff. Teachers should, however, be willing to work with whatever space is available.

Infection Control. Infection control plays an important and often high profile role in health care settings. Classes taught in hospitals or clinics will be subject to strict infection control policies that may impact the types of props that can be used. When beginning a new program, yoga teachers should request a briefing on infection control policy from a local POC and respect guidelines at all times.

Time Management. Punctuality—beginning and ending yoga classes on time—is key in maintaining a sense of safety, predictability, and control for students. In addition, yoga participants may have follow-up appointments after class. The yoga room may also be needed for other purposes immediately following the designated end time.

It is critical to establish who is responsible for class set-up and breakdown prior to the start of the program. Any problems with this arrangement should be immediately reported to the POC.

TEACHING IN THE VA 2: Adapt to Meet Medical Needs

Yoga teachers working in medical settings should be sensitive to the variety of limitations or challenges that individual students may have, and adjust teaching accordingly.

Teachers working in VA Medical Centers or other clinical settings should learn about students' medical challenges. This is not to suggest they seek to become self-taught doctors, nurses, or therapists; as discussed in the "Teaching and Curriculum Best Practices" section, teachers must maintain strict professional boundaries. A basic knowledge about students' core challenges helps teachers adapt yoga classes to meet their needs and provide the most healing, empowering experience possible. Teachers should also be sensitive to potential privacy concerns and remain in compliance with HIPAA at all times.

As discussed in the "Best Practices for Working with Trauma" and "Staffing and Training Best Practices" sections, all yoga teachers working with veterans should be trained in trauma-informed yoga. Those working in hospitals and clinical settings should ideally have more extensive yoga teacher training (RYT 500 status or equivalent), at least five years of teaching experience, a high level of personal maturity, and additional specialized training as necessary to meet particular student needs, such as working with traumatic brain injuries (TBIs), PTSD, chronic pain, and mobility impairments.

Yoga teachers should take care to follow any applicable rules and procedures carefully. For example, they should know and strictly adhere to policies regarding ID badging, infection control, local SOPs (standard operating procedures), and privacy (HIPAA, or Health Insurance Portability and Accountability Act regulations). When teaching in a hospital setting and working with an injured participant, they should always ensure a staff member is present (e.g., PT or OT) to assist in transitioning in and out of class. Any problems coordinating with staff should be immediately discussed with the POC and, if applicable, an external contracting agency supervisor.

Specialized Medical Needs. It is beyond the scope of this book to discuss the wide variety of medical needs that yoga teachers may encounter when working in a VA Medical Center or other clinical setting. The following discussion covers special considerations for working with veterans with medical conditions requiring the utilization of mobility devices, service dogs, and medications. This is only an introduction to the vast terrain of specialized medical needs. This information is presented to inform interested teachers, students, or facilitators, not as a substitute for professional expertise or training.

Assistive Mobility Devices. Individuals with decreased function of their lower extremities receive benefit from a variety of assistive devices including braces, canes, crutches, walkers, or prostheses in the case of amputations. Further decline warrants the use of a manual wheelchair, as it is versatile, lightweight, and easily transported. In cases with generalized weakness, loss of balance, and significant fatigue, a powered mobility device such as a scooter (similar to those seen in grocery stores), or a motorized wheelchair may be more appropriate.

To be evaluated for power mobility device, a veteran requires a referral from their VA primary care provider to a physical therapist (PT), occupational therapist (OT), or facility wheelchair clinic to determine eligibility. Once options are discussed, the best device (appropriately customized) is ordered and delivered. The process can take several months. The clinic then provides fitting of the device and training sessions to learn to use the mobility device.

Yoga teachers working in the VA should be prepared to teach students both in standard chairs and wheelchairs. It's important to remember, however, that in many cases, veterans utilizing wheelchairs and other assistive devices may be able to do poses without them. In such cases, students will know how to transfer in and out of the chair themselves. It is not expected that the yoga teacher will help them to do this. Instructors should, however, clarify this with the students and the POC.

Inpatient hospitalization settings may present different situations. Students may be weak from illness, or in the process of learning to operate their mobility device. In such cases, a staff member may accompany a patient to class. They, and not the yoga teacher, will be in charge of any transfers in and out of the chair. They may also be able to help encourage the patient in certain poses, and get feedback on activity limitations.

In all cases, the yoga teacher should be sure that motorized wheelchairs are in the "off" position when near a student – they are quite heavy, and make for sore feet when they run over them!

Service Dogs. With the long duration of recent conflicts in Iraq (OIF) and Afghanistan (OEF) and increasing numbers of wounded and injured, VAs have been exploring alternative methods of therapy beyond medications, including the use of service dogs. Yoga teachers working in VAs should be prepared for the possibility that veterans may bring a service dog to class.

Service dogs fall under the category of "working dogs," which includes police dogs, search and rescue dogs, detection dogs (for sniffing out drugs, arson, and explosives), military guard dogs, herding dogs, and hunting mates. Service animals are highly trained, and enjoy certain rights and protections under the Americans with Disabilities Act (ADA), which yoga teachers should be aware of. The ADA recognizes five types of medical service dogs: mobility dogs, medical alert dogs,[34] guide dogs, dogs for hearing impaired, and psychological service dogs.

Training usually begins when the dogs are puppies, and takes two years. This timeframe is due to the complexity and intensity of the training, as well as the need to allow the dog to naturally mature. Part of the training can include a period of several months with their handler (the terms "patient" or "client" are not used). Training is rigorous, and exclusively conducted by certified schools. Animals that complete training are formally certified, and given documentation.

Two other categories of dogs are often seen in the healthcare setting: emotional support animals (ESA) and therapy animals (usually, but not necessarily dogs). ESAs have no specific training, as their purpose is to provide comfort by their mere existence. To be eligible, veterans need a letter from their physician stating they need an ESA for disability support. ESAs are often allowed in healthcare settings. Therapy animals, in contrast, work with nondisabled handlers to provide comfort to others. Unlike medical service dogs, they have no legal right to be admitted to public spaces. Typically, however, therapy animals are granted permission to visit hospitals and nursing homes.

Yoga teachers should be aware that the VA and DOD each have their own specific service animal policies. Generally, they mimic the ADA's. There may, however, be specific local variances. Some VA Medical Centers may have Animal Assisted Therapy Programs, including therapy dogs. Currently, there are studies ongoing to assess and improve their value at USUHS (the Uniformed Services University of the Health Sciences). It is anticipated that policy will change in response to this research.

Best practices with regard to service animals include the following:

---

34 Medical alert dogs work with individuals who have significant metabolic disabilities such as unstable diabetes or seizures. Medical alert dogs are able to detect subtle biochemical changes in their handler 25-30 minutes prior to an event, and will alert their handler to take preventive action. The alert may be in the form of a nudge for a soft vocalization.

- When dogs are with their handlers in a public setting, they are highly focused and working. In general, wearing a vest signals to the dog and those around him that he is in working status.
- Never pet or feed service dogs without asking permission.
- Absent extenuating circumstances, service animals should be permitted in yoga classes in VA settings, even if there is no ADA requirement to do so (as in the case of an ESA). Animals must be under the control of the handler and toilet trained. If these conditions are not met, it is OK to ask both to leave. If the student wants to come back to class without the animal, they should be allowed to do so.
- If a student brings a service animal to a yoga class, the teacher should confer with the handler/student before deciding where it is best to position them.
- If a yoga student has a medical alert dog, the teacher should ask what the alert is before class starts. This will help the teacher be prepared to assist the student, if necessary, and help the class run smoothly.

Medications. As veterans age, they are subject to the same acute and chronic medical issues as the U.S. population as a whole. Yoga students may be on medications for high blood pressure, diabetes, elevated cholesterol, thyroid conditions, and other health issues—just as in a regular community yoga class. Yoga teachers should inquire about injuries and other health concerns and remind students to practice self-care, listen to their bodies, and pace themselves appropriately.

In VA Medical Centers and other clinical settings, there may be a much higher percentage of individuals taking medication for complications of traumatic brain injury (TBI), mTBI (mild traumatic brain injury) and/or PTSD than in the general population. Difficulty with sleep, agitation, labile moods, and poor impulse control are often associated with these diagnoses. Students may be on medications, or in the process of having medications adjusted. Those with physical injuries often also have both acute and chronic pain for which they may be prescribed narcotics, among many other drugs.[35]

Although an in depth discussion of individual medications and their side effects is beyond the scope of this publication, some helpful generalizations concerning the *groups of medications seen in high frequency in VA settings* can be made.[36] These include:

- Anti-depressants,
- medications for diabetes and hypertension (including diuretics),
- anti-convulsants or seizure medications,
- neuroleptics (anti-psychotic medications),
- narcotic and non-narcotic analgesics (pain medications), and
- anxiolytics (anti-anxiety medications).

Most of these medications can have a slowing effect on cognition; i.e., the process of acquiring knowledge and understanding via thought, experience, and the senses. Students may be sleepy, drowsy, and sluggish, or even have a tendency to doze. For those who have been used to being high functioning, this can be irritating and embarrassing. These feelings, in turn, contribute even more frustration to that caused by the underlying conditions for which the medications were prescribed.

Many veterans are exploring yoga and other alternative and complementary methods as potential tools to help decrease their dependence on medication and support their overall well-being. The VA and the DOD have officially recognized

35 Extensive work is being done both within VA and externally to determine how chronic pain might be managed while reducing or eliminating the use of opioids, which have problematic side effects and are highly addictive. For a helpful overview of this issue, see Gallagher (2016).

36 These generalizations are anecdotal, based on the knowledge and experience of Contributors to this volume. They are intended only to provide guidance to yoga teachers, and should not be construed to represent VA policy or scientific data.

this, and are supporting greater dissemination of yoga, meditation, and other integrative medical practices in an attempt to help maximize quality of life and, as appropriate, decrease the polypharmacy historically seen in these populations. Given the many anecdotal reports of success from VA facilities nationwide, it is reasonable to expect that increasing the number of quality yoga classes for veterans will prove enormously helpful in this regard.

Teaching Cognitively Impaired Students. It may be challenging to teach yoga students who have various levels of cognitive impairment, including side effects from medications or other health conditions. To do so effectively requires teachers to be grounded in their own practice, engage in self-care, and cultivate supportive relationships with peers and other professionals (see the "Relationship Building Best Practices" section). It may take several classes for teachers to truly understand each student's functional level. Teachers should be careful not to take student irritability or other challenging behaviors personally.

Teachers should be aware that HIPAA privacy regulations prohibit non-medical personnel from accessing medical data in a medical setting. HIPAA also holds that private health information cannot be discussed in a public setting where others may overhear it. While a student may volunteer information about medications, the teacher should not ask.

In groups with individuals who are taking many medications or have significant cognitive challenges, classes should be taught slowly and with clear, crisp, precise language. Teachers should give no more than three instructions at one time, and avoid flowery language and long explanations. This is especially important if there are students with TBI, PTSD, mood disorders, or cognitive processing challenges related to medication or other mental or physical health issues.

Since many commonly prescribed medications have the side effect of dry mouth, it is good to suggest that students bring a closed water bottle to class. If students are new to yoga, teachers may need to point out that coffee and/or energy drinks are not appropriate, and explain why.

Many of these medications can affect the cardiovascular system in ways that prevent the body from efficiently regulating blood pressure and heart rate. This may produce orthostatic hypotension, a transient lowering of blood pressure caused by moving quickly from a seated or prone to standing position. This condition can lead to lightheadedness or fainting, so teachers should be cautious with any transitions. Many of these medications also affect the central nervous system, and can cause side effects of dizziness or unsteadiness. These two symptoms, however, can also be related to underlying injuries.

Nonetheless, it remains useful for students to practice balance poses. The teacher should observe them carefully, however, to make such poses appropriately challenging, neither overly frustrating nor easy. Teachers may also wish to suggest to students that practicing balancing poses, in which it's common to fall out of place and need to begin again, offers a valuable opportunity for self-study and the practice of nonjudgmental awareness.

TEACHING IN THE VA 3: Conduct Program Evaluations

Yoga teachers working in the VA should conduct program evaluations on a regular basis.

Program evaluation can play a valuable role in helping teachers fine-tune their class offerings, while collecting data to help support and promote future work. Teachers should be aware, however, that many government agencies have formal processes and regulations for program evaluation. Teachers should work with their local POC to discuss evaluation options.

Some VA locations express concerns about veterans being "over-surveyed" and only allow officially sanctioned evaluations. In such settings, informal methods are advised and acceptable: e.g., tracking attendance, collecting student feedback on class benefits, and conducting a simple assessment of how students feel before and after class using the DOD/VA pain scale. (The latter is particularly valuable as it is a recognized and reproducible tool.) If student surveys are permitted, they should be quick, simple, and replicable, and include both quantitative and qualitative measures.

As noted in the "Relationship Building Best Practices" section, giving anonymous surveys to solicit student feedback on their experience in class, and with yoga overall, can play an important role in strengthening the teacher-student relationship. Establishing such open feedback loops shows students that their thoughts and feelings are valued, and keeps communication channels fully open in ways that facilitate improving the class experience for all.

BEST PRACTICES FOR TEACHING INCARCERATED VETERANS

The U.S. incarcerates more of its citizens than any other country in the world. With only four percent of the world population, it accounts for 25 percent of all prisoners globally. Approximately 2.25 million adults are imprisoned in 4,575 American correctional facilities, 600,000 of them for non-violent, drug-related offenses. Roughly 92 percent of these prisoners are male; 8 percent are female. With a recidivism rate of 60 percent, the U.S. system is a revolving door, with 6 of 10 offenders returning to prison within three years of their release (Warren, 2008; Lennard, 2012).

Prior to 2000, only a few yoga classes—typically emphasizing traditional yoga philosophy—existed in prisons. Since then, numerous organizations dedicated to offering a more secular, psycho-physiological, therapeutic approach have emerged. Nationally, an estimated 150-175 jails and prisons have yoga classes provided by outside program providers (i.e., individual yoga teachers and/or yoga service organizations). These jail and prison yoga providers are most heavily concentrated in state and county correctional facilities located on the East and West Coasts. A handful of classes are also offered at federal institutions. Most of these organizations specialize in teaching either youth or adults, and either male or female populations. Additionally, an estimated 50-75 correctional facilities allow prisoner-led classes.

Approximately 10 percent of incarcerated adults in the U.S. are veterans (Noonan and Mumola, 2007). This population typically suffers from the same forms of trauma as non-incarcerated veterans, although it may be more pronounced and untreated. Incarcerated veterans also deal with additional traumas incurred by incarceration.

Field reports indicate that there is both a need, and a widespread request to develop veterans-only yoga classes in prisons. Often, the sense of community and support from other veterans such classes facilitate goes a long way towards helping individuals find comfort and release.

TEACHING INCARCERATED VETERANS 1: CONSIDER PROGRAM REQUIREMENTS

Understand the importance of provider structure, administrative location, point of contact, screening processes, rules and regulations, and funding options when developing a prison yoga program.

It is beyond the scope of this book to provide a detailed discussion of how to develop a yoga program for incarcerated veterans from scratch. The following points, however, are important to consider in launching this process.

- *Individual or Organization.* Thought should be given as to how best to approach prison officials, including whether to present oneself as an individual, or part of an established organization. Generally speaking, it is easier to set up a new program in affiliation with an established organization, ideally one that specializes in yoga for veterans and/or the incarcerated. In many cases, however, correctional facilities will be open to individually-directed programs. What makes the most sense will vary according to geographic location, institutional leadership, and teacher preference.

- *Administrative Location.* It is important to determine whether a new yoga program will be administered through Voluntary Services, or some other contracting department (e.g., Recreation, Rehabilitation, or Reentry). This will impact both the teacher screening and institutional orientation processes, and whether an instructor or organization can be compensated.

- *Point of Contact.* As in the case of starting a new yoga program in the VA, it is ideal to cultivate a relationship with an "internal champion." Finding this person may take some work, and will not always be possible. Increasingly, however, wardens or unit managers may be interested in bringing yoga into their facility after reading about yoga for prisoners in the news, or learning about a prison yoga provider on the Internet.

  As in the case of the VA, it is critical to be able to explain the benefits of yoga for incarcerated veterans in accessible, concise, compelling terms, appropriately adopted to fit the available audience, time frame, and setting.

- *Screening.* Find out what vetting requirements (background checks, TB tests, fingerprinting, etc.) must be fulfilled before beginning a program. Although every institution will likely require something different, virtually all mandate background checks and facility orientation training. Some, but not all institutions require fingerprints. The process can range from a few days to several months. If a program is set up at a VA facility, TB testing will most likely be required.

  Individual clearances will likely be required for each prison where a yoga program is being established. While it is possible to obtain a statewide prison clearance, instructors are generally required to submit a new application and background check for each facility.

  The screening process can often be lengthy and frustrating. Yoga instructors should be aware that this clearance process may be as challenging as any yoga practice, requiring mindfulness and patience.

- *Rules and Procedures.* Teaching in a jail or prison requires strict adherence to all institutional regulations, approval processes, and protocols. Each correctional facility will have its own training or orientation concerning these matters for "outside" or "free staff" program providers. Even if the stated rules do not always seem to be enforced, follow them anyway. Any infraction is cause for ending the program, and should be scrupulously avoided.

- *Funding.* It is extremely rare for a yoga program to be funded by the facility, or the county, state, or federal government. Those interested in teaching yoga to incarcerated veterans should be prepared to undertake the classes as "karma yoga," or selfless service through yoga for the good of all, including oneself.

TEACHING INCARCERATED VETERANS 2: PROVIDE CONSISTENCY

Yoga teachers should coordinate with co-teachers and substitute teachers to provide a consistent classroom experience.

Consistency is key to establishing a successful yoga program for incarcerated veterans. Simply offering a reliable time and space to attend class is a big part of its value. This is particularly true given the likelihood that a high percentage of students had disrupted lives before incarceration, and the certainty that all are now experiencing powerlessness in a correctional environment.

To further support consistency in class offerings, all yoga teachers should have at least one qualified co-teacher who attends and facilitates class with them, as well as a substitute teacher who is able to teach if necessary. Substitute teachers must be pre-approved by the facility in order to be able to enter and teach when needed, so it's important to plan ahead.

TEACHING INCARCERATED VETERANS 3: CONSIDER GENDER DYNAMICS

Consider the gender match between teachers and students, and the possibility of using a male/female teaching team.

While approximately 92 percent of the incarcerated population is male, 80 percent of yoga practitioners are women (FBP 2016; Medlin, 2014). Consequently, female yoga teachers interested in working with incarcerated veterans will most likely face the question of whether to teach men. Should they choose to do so, they should be prepared to deal with gender-related issues, and take precautions as necessary to ensure their safety.

Some experts in the field believe that the ideal teaching team for incarcerated veterans consists of a man and a woman. Practicing and modeling a non-hierarchical, respectful, and professional mixed-gender relationship can be a beneficial practice for teachers and students alike. In such cases, teachers should carefully think through issues such as setting boundaries, clothing choices, and teaching terminology together (see the "Teaching and Curriculum Best Practices" section, above).

TEACHING INCARCERATED VETERANS 4: USE TIME WISELY

Teachers should prepare ahead, arrive early, expect schedule disruptions, and be prepared to modify class plans as necessary.

The teacher's yoga practice should start as soon as they get in the car to drive to class. Teaching in a correctional facility requires being prepared for the unexpected, and being willing to let go of any plans and expectations. Teachers must be ready to adapt as necessary to work with whatever is happening that day at the institution.

Although it is unlikely that teachers will encounter a physically dangerous situation, prisons can be chaotic, unpredictable environments. It is useful to set an intention to remain alert, and take a few minutes to mentally prepare before entering.

Generally speaking, it is best to arrive 20-30 minutes before the start time of the class. Teachers should allow plenty of time to pass through the security system and checkpoints. They should always plan to start and end classes on time, regardless of whether or not this actually occurs.

Schedule disruptions such as prison lockdowns and class cancellations may occur at any time. Teachers should be prepared to adjust their class plans accordingly. There are often unexpected changes to the amount of time you will be able to teach. Teachers should arrive prepared to offer a "complete" yoga class (with an opening; integrated mind, breath and movement core; and final meditation/relaxation), regardless of how much time actually ends up being available.

Teachers should also be aware of any additional time commitments related to program management. For example, there may be paperwork requirements such release forms, intake forms, and questionnaires. Teachers should understand what's required of them and cooperate with program managers and/or facility administrators to ensure that paperwork is consistently complete and up-to-date. Ideally, such record-keeping will be utilized to support the quality and ongoing viability of the program.

TEACHING INCARCERATED VETERANS 5: DRESS APPROPRIATELY

Teachers entering a correctional facility should take extra care to dress appropriately.

As discussed in the "Teaching and Curriculum Best Practices" sections, yoga teachers working with veterans should dress more conservatively than is the norm at fitness centers and yoga studios. These norms should be followed when teaching in a correctional facility, in addition to the following clothing considerations:

- Wear loose-fitting clothes free of writing and logos.
- Wear layers that can be removed as needed in response to movement or heat without exposing skin.
- Always wear undergarments (this may be required by the facility).

- Wear a watch (there may not be a clock available, and phones won't be allowed inside the facility).
- If jewelry is worn, do not have necklaces or dangly earrings.
- Wear close-toed shoes.
- Check facility requirements to see whether wearing hooded sweatshirts is permissible.
- It is common for facilities to prohibit volunteers from wearing the same color as inmates. In general, choose clothing colors that stand out, rather than blend in. This is safer for both teacher and students.

TEACHING INCARCERATED VETERANS 6: MANAGE PERSONAL ITEMS AND YOGA PROPS

Do not bring personal items (other than required ID and car keys) or yoga props inside a facility without pre-approval of each item and access to a secure storage location.

Yoga teachers should never transport any unauthorized materials into or out of a correctional facility.

Very few personal items are allowed inside and, in most cases, teachers will not be allowed to bring in anything other than their ID badge and car keys. Cell phones will likely not be allowed. Large key chains should be detached from car keys and left with other personal items in the trunk. Alternatively, some facilities may have lockers available for teachers to store personal items.

Anything a teacher wants to bring into a class must be pre-approved. This includes simple items such as pens, pencils, papers, and books. Some—but not all—facilities may allow the distribution of pre-approved informational handouts on yoga for students (who are often interested). Anything with staples will not be approved. If handouts are allowed, do not assume that the facility will make copies. Any recording devices, including cameras, will require pre-authorization.

If teachers wish to play music, all necessary items will require pre-approval. (See "Teaching and Curriculum Best Practices" for the pros and cons of music in class.) The best arrangement, if allowed, is to leave a simple CD player and CDs (or the equivalent) in a secure location in the facility that can be easily accessed by teachers.

If teachers wish to use yoga props in class, most likely they will need to:

- have their use pre-approved by the facility,
- find a way to buy or have them donated, and
- arrange for a secure, pre-approved storage location.

Mats and other props may unexpectedly go missing. If this occurs, it should be immediately reported to the program manager.

TEACHING INCARCERATED VETERANS 7: ESTABLISH SAFE SPACE

Yoga teachers should work with facility administrators to create a safe space for the class.

While yoga teachers working in correctional facilities should be prepared for unexpected room changes, they should also do whatever they can in advance to ensure a safe classroom space. Recommended actions include:

- *Know safety procedures.* Yoga teachers should attend all orientations and trainings provided by the facility, and understand all relevant safety rules and procedures.

- *Know the room.* If possible, teachers should visit the classroom before teaching in it. Lesson plans should be designed to work with available space and props effectively.
- *Maximize cleanliness.* Ask the institution ahead of time about the condition of the room and where cleaning supplies are kept. Although you can ask for a clean and uncluttered room, do not assume that it will be clean or clutter-free.
- *Plan student placement.* If possible, teachers should arrange the physical layout of the classroom so that students are in a circle or oval with their backs to the wall. That way there is no one behind them, and they can see everyone present.
- *Teach trauma-informed yoga.* Classes for incarcerated veterans should follow previously discussed protocols for teaching trauma-informed yoga (see the "Best Practices for Working with Trauma" section).
- *Do not touch students.* In keeping with a trauma-informed method, teachers should refrain from touching students or giving pose "adjustments." In a correctional setting, this "no touch" rule goes beyond yoga instruction to include all interpersonal interactions. Even a post-class handshake could be misinterpreted by prisoners and/or staff, and is best avoided.
- *Cooperate with staff.* Teachers should work to secure the support of custody staff, and be mindful and appreciative that their main purpose is "care and control" to maintain safety in the institution.
- *Have emergency support.* Yoga teachers should know where facility support personnel are at all times. These arrangements will vary with each institution. They should also know where to go in case of an emergency and how to sound an alarm if necessary. If permissible, teachers should carry a whistle.
- *Follow exit procedures.* Each facility will have different rules regarding exit procedures. Teachers should know what the rules are, and follow

them. Most facilities will require the instructor to be escorted out by a correctional officer.

TEACHING INCARCERATED VETERANS 8: INTEGRATE AUTHENTICITY AND PROFESSIONALISM

Yoga teachers should strive to connect authentically with students, while rigorously maintaining personal and professional boundaries.

As in any yoga class, it is important for teachers to establish a rapport with their students in an authentic way. Unless a teacher has been incarcerated and can speak to that experience directly, it's best to focus on emphasizing the therapeutic benefits of yoga. If the teacher happens to be a veteran, it's important to share that information. Ideally, teachers can speak to the personal benefits they have gained from the practice, particularly as it pertains to their military background and training, and active duty or combat experience.

Veterans often share a strong bond as a result of their service. As a result, they often exhibit a certain exclusivity vis-à-vis civilians. It may take a while for teachers without military experience to establish a connection with students. Civilian males in particular may have to earn their respect and trust by exhibiting qualities of leadership and integrity. This could mean simply being consistent with one's word and following through, or taking initiative in the classroom if there is any confusion or disagreement.

Cultural obstacles often prevent true listening between military personnel and civilians. Of course, this is not always the case, and experience indicates that the number of exceptions is increasing. Yoga teachers who are not familiar with the military, however, should be committed to learning about it from their students on an ongoing basis. Cultivating an atmosphere of open-mindedness and respect is particularly important given that many incarcerated veterans may be unfamiliar with yoga, and view it as a foreign and perhaps questionable practice.

Regardless of what common ground is established, it is imperative to maintain personal and professional boundaries at all times for the safety and benefit of both teacher and students. Teachers should communicate on a first name (as opposed to full name) basis, and resist sharing personal information.

TEACHING INCARCERATED VETERANS 9: COMMUNICATE CLASS RULES AND OBJECTIVES

Yoga teachers should set clear ground rules for students while listening to their experiences, and set class objectives that speak to them directly.

When teaching incarcerated veterans, it is helpful to set simple class rules, and explain them to the class. For example, are the participants allowed to leave class to use the restroom? Must they stay for the entire class? Is talking allowed during the practice? How will student questions be addressed? Rules need to be clearly established and consistently applied. Of course, all class rules must follow those of the facility.

It is helpful for teachers to speak directly to the overall objectives for the class: e.g., calming the mind, relieving stress, and improving mind/body health. Teachers should be ready and able to reference benefits reported by veterans and prisoners who have embraced a yoga practice, such as improved sleep, self-control/impulse control, emotional stability, and clearer focus and thinking. They can also acknowledge that yoga can help cultivate an internal sense of personal power and space, which is often unavailable in the external environment of a jail or prison.

It's important to establish a context for yoga that's relevant to the students' lives in an incarcerated environment, and as veterans. Teachers should be receptive to what students say about their experiences, and allow that information to guide their teaching. In general, it's best to present yoga in ways that are relevant to the issues students are dealing with, without making assumptions about what those issues might be.

TEACHING INCARCERATED VETERANS 10: ENCOURAGE SELF-SENSITIVITY AND SELF-CARE

Yoga classes should provide students with tools, resources, and encouragement for developing self-sensitivity and practicing self-care.

Most prisoners have personal histories that include what's clinically known as "complex trauma." This phrase refers to both the occurrence and effects of children's exposure to multiple traumatic events, often of a severe, invasive, and interpersonal nature, such as abuse or profound neglect.

Psychologists agree that trauma that begins early in life can disrupt many aspects of child development, including the formation of a core sense of self. When, as is most often the case, chronic trauma occurs in the context of a child's relationship with a primary caregiver, it interferes with the child's ability to form a secure attachment bond. This loss of security and stability early in life has profoundly negative effects on many aspects of children's physical and mental development (NCTSN, 2016).

In the case of incarcerated veterans, the ongoing effects of complex trauma can be exacerbated by unresolved trauma experienced in the military. Both may be further compounded by trauma associated with incarceration. Addiction and mental health issues are often deeply enmeshed with such accumulated trauma. It is estimated that 80 percent of all prisoners struggle with addiction to alcohol and/or drugs.

Many incarcerated veterans are also grappling with conditions such as hyper-arousal, poor impulse control, and an inability to concentrate/focus. Anxiety, depression and despair are rife. Prisoners tend to lack a healthy association with their bodies, a condition commonly associated with unresolved trauma and/or having lived a criminal lifestyle. This experience of physical self-disassociation is often is manifested by "armoring," "muscling up," and otherwise hardening oneself to increase physical and emotional protection.

Given these considerations, yoga classes for incarcerated veterans should be structured to facilitate reconnecting with the physical and emotional body in a sensitive way. Overly vigorous, "workout"-style practices should be avoided. Instead, yoga teachers should aim to increase physical strength by lengthening muscles and becoming more flexible, while developing mind/body integration and building psychological resilience.

Class themes such as working with "effortless effort" can be used to invite students to explore the middle ground between exertion and relaxation. Eventually, this felt sense of internal balance allows students to discover that real strength comes from a deep connection with their inner selves. Developing this sense of deep, authentic self-connection allows them to gradually and safely unwind any hard-wired sense of needing to be constantly "on alert." All aspects of the class, including movement, conscious breathing, meditation, and relaxation, should be utilized to skillfully encourage self-sensitivity and self-care.

TEACHING INCARCERATED VETERANS 11: PROCESS EMOTIONS

Teachers should take care to process their personal emotions consciously and constructively as part of an ongoing commitment to self-care.

Teachers should be aware that teaching in a jail or prison often generates strong emotions. These may run the gamut from intense feelings of inner peace to rage. It is important for instructors to be as aware of their feelings as they can, so that they can develop a process for releasing them. Techniques to enable emotional release might include talking with a friend or loved one, physical movement, yogic breathing exercises, or meditation.

Ideally, this emotional cleansing should be done immediately after class, before continuing on with the day. It is necessary, however, for the instructor to leave the entire facility, including the parking lot, before turning attention to this process. Teachers should be certain that they have a safe space to take some time for themselves, whether in their car or some other off-site location. It will likely take some time to decompress, re-ground, and reconnect to the present moment. Maintaining a consistent self-care routine is critical to doing this work effectively, and avoiding burnout. (See the "Relationship Building Best Practices" section for a further discussion of self-care issues.)

BEST PRACTICES FOR WORKING WITH FAMILIES OF VETERANS

Since the advent of the all-volunteer force in the 1970s, marriage, parenthood, and family life have become much more prevalent in the U.S. Armed Forces. Military spouses and children now outnumber service members by a ratio of 1.4 to 1.[37] Given that the average length of service is seven years, this translates into large numbers of veteran family members. In 2011, for example, approximately 184,000 people left the military. At a rate of 1.4 family members per service member, this means that more than 250,000 military family members became veteran family members (Clever and Segal, 2013).

Segal (1986) influentially characterized both the military and the family as "greedy" institutions, in that both demand intense levels of commitment, time, and energy, making it difficult to participate actively in other life roles. From this perspective, military families are faced with the double whammy of negotiating two such demanding institutions at once. Although the military also offers substantial benefits to families, the consequent level of stress faced by military families is generally high.

Family Stressors. Two of the biggest stressors for military families are adjusting to long deployments and frequent moves. Of course, having a family member absent is stressful in and of itself. Military-specific stressors, such as knowing that a family member may be in hostile territory,

---

37 In 2011, 726,500 spouses and more than 1.2 million dependent children lived in active-duty families, and 409,801 spouses and 743,736 dependent children lived in Guard and Reserve families (Clever and Segal, 2013).

compounds that stress. Not surprisingly, research indicates that longer periods of deployment correlate with higher divorce rates. This is particularly true for female service members married to civilian men, and couples who married before 9/11 and were then unexpectedly swept into the increased rate of post-9/11 deployment (Negrusa et al, 2014).

Active duty military personnel typically move once every two to three years, 2.4 times the rate of civilian families. Military families are also more likely to move long distances, across state lines, or to foreign countries. While the need to repeatedly re-establish life in new places is stressful for military personnel and their families alike, their experiences of it are necessarily different. Upon moving, service members are immediately connected to familiar work structures and a new military community. Family members, in contrast, must negotiate the challenges of forging new work, school, and community arrangements and connections in more varied, unfamiliar contexts.

Yoga classes crafted to meet the needs, concerns, and values of military and veteran families provide a potentially important source of support to family members, and, by extension, to military members and veterans themselves. Family systems theory details what many people understand from experience: The family is an emotional unit, and individuals within it are interconnected and interdependent. Serving veterans in meaningful ways necessarily requires supporting their families as well.

WORKING WITH FAMILIES OF VETERANS 1: DEFINE "FAMILY" INCLUSIVELY

Recognize and respect the diversity of family structures that exist in the military and among veterans today, as well as the variety of relationships that may constitute "family."

Despite steady increases since the 1970s in the percentage of women who serve, the armed forces remain overwhelmingly male. This means that the vast majority of military spouses are female (93%), and that the majority of military parents are fathers. Most military spouses are also civilians.

The most common family structure is that of a military man married to a civilian woman. Many others exist, including categories that are common in civilian life (e.g., single parents, same-sex couples), as well as one unique to the military—the "dual-service" couple, in which both partners are service members.

Although many male service members are involved in non-traditional family structures, females are disproportionately represented in this group. For example, in absolute numbers, there are more male-headed single parent families among active duty and reserve personnel than female-headed ones. Women, however, are still disproportionately likely to be single parents. While comprising 14.6% of the active duty and 18.2% of reserve components, they represent 30% of the military single parent population. Women service members are also more likely to be divorced, unmarried, and/or part of dual-service and stepparent families (Southwell and Wadsworth, 2016).[38]

In addition to the diverse family structures that exist among active duty personnel, reservists, and veterans today, it is important to consider the full range of relationships that may be involved in creating a meaningful sense of family. In addition to spouses, partners and children, this may include caregivers, non-medical attendants (NMAs), siblings, grandparents, cousins, aunts and uncles, close friends, work colleagues, and pets.

WORKING WITH FAMILIES OF VETERANS 2: RECOGNIZE DIVERSE FAMILY NEEDS

Yoga teachers and program administrators should seek to learn about the diverse needs and concerns of military and veteran families in the communities they serve.

38 While dual-military marriages represent a small portion of active duty (11.3%) and selected reserve component (5.5%) marriages, women are over 7 times more likely to be part of dual-military families than men. This ratio varies significantly by service branch. For example, women serving in the Coast Guard and Marine Corps reserve are more than 16 times more likely to be married to other service members (Clever and Segal, 2013).

Yoga teachers and program administrators seeking to serve military and veteran families should consider how best to structure classes to meet the diverse needs and concerns of the families in the community they are serving. Of course, the best way to learn what is needed is by engaging with people on the ground. Certain categories of differential needs and concerns, however, can be anticipated in advance. These include both different types of families, and families encountering different stages of the military career cycle.

Stages of Deployment. While most service members spend their entire careers training for deployments, family members and friends do not (unless they are members of the military themselves). Typically, family, friends, supportive community members, and even service providers are not trained to handle the emotional challenges of the deployment experience.

The full spectrum of emotions that accompany a military deployment cycle also tends to be grossly misunderstood. Working with it effectively requires not just looking at post-deployment reintegration, but also the pre-deployment, deployment, and reunion periods. Yoga teachers working with active duty personnel should be sensitive to the emotional challenges associated with each part of this cycle, while understanding that different individuals and families cope with these emotional challenges in different ways.[39]

National Guard and Reserve Families. Families of National Guardsmen and Reservists face distinct challenges. Typically, these families live in civilian communities, and are much more dispersed geographically than active duty families. The resultant isolation from others who share their military experiences may be challenging not only for service men and women, but their family members as well.

Further, these families face unique challenges around deployment. Members of the National Guard and Reserves are only paid by the military when deployed. Otherwise, they are expected to participate in the civilian labor force. Given their

39 For a helpful discussion of these issues, see Blue Star Families/Vulcan Productions, 2013.

increased rate of deployment during the post 9/11 era, as well the impact of 2008 economic crisis, this arrangement has greatly intensified the stress surrounding employment issues for these service members and their families.[40]

Civilian Husbands. Civilian men married to military women face particular challenges. Research indicates that most of these men believe that military activities and support resources are not designed to meet their needs. They also report feeling stigmatized by any use of support resources, and isolated from the military and civilian communities alike. Civilian husbands tend to shy away from activities designed for military spouses, reporting that it's difficult to connect with groups primarily composed of military wives. Although the military has made some changes to try to better accommodate male spouses, a perception that civilian husbands of military wives are "oddities" remains widespread (Southwell and Wadsworth, 2016).

WORKING WITH FAMILIES OF VETERANS 3: CARE FOR THE CAREGIVERS

Offer care to military caregivers by providing tools for stress reduction, and support for self-care.

Many veterans rely on informal caregivers for daily, long-term support beyond what the VA and social services provide. These military caregivers are typically spouses, parents, children, or other relatives. In some cases, they are friends and neighbors.

Military caregivers provide assistance with tasks of daily living (e.g., eating, walking), offer mental and emotional support, help navigate the health care system, and assist with legal and financial matters.[41] According to a 2014 RAND study, the 5.5 million military caregivers in the U.S. today are best understood

40 For an in-depth examination of the particular challenges facing National Guard and Reservist families, see Castaneda et al, 2008.

41 This section is based on the findings of Ramchand et al, 2014.

in terms of two distinct groups: those caring for veterans who served in the military before, and after 9/11.

Pre-9/11 Caregivers. A majority of pre-9/11 veterans receiving informal care fit the profile of an elderly person with needs related to aging. Almost a third (30 percent) also have disabilities related to their military service.

About 80 percent of military caregivers, or 4.4 million people, are caring for veterans from the pre-9/11 era. In many respects, these caregivers resemble their civilian counterparts. Typically, they are either adult children caring for an aging parent, or a spouse caring for a partner. Nearly 90 percent are older than 30. Almost half are older than 55. Over half are retired or otherwise unemployed. A large majority of pre-9/11 caregivers can draw on a network of family and friends for support.

Post-9/11 Caregivers. The number of veterans with disabling injuries or illnesses has spiked sharply since the advent of OEF and OIF. Most of these veterans are young. Nearly two-thirds have mental health or substance use disorders, including PTSD, depression, and anxiety. One-fifth have traumatic brain injuries—roughly twice the rate of pre-9/11 care recipients. Consequently, those caring for these veterans typically spend less time on elderly caregiving. Instead, they focus on helping their loved one cope with stressful situations, including triggers that spike anxiety or provoke anti-social behavior.

Nearly 90 percent of post-9/11 caregivers are 55 or younger, and over a third are 30 or younger. Most commonly, they are young spouses and/or parents with young children. A surprisingly large number are friends or neighbors, including wartime buddies caring for wounded comrades. Nearly two-thirds are employed, and 40 percent are raising at least one child. Unlike their pre-9/11 counterparts, a majority of these caregivers lack a social network capable of supporting them.

Caregiver Stress. All military caregivers are coping with substantial demands and stress. Between 50-60 percent spend at least ten hours per week providing care. Spouses typically provide an additional 14 hours per week beyond that.

Despite or because of these demands, military caregivers often tend to neglect their own physical and mental health. Their health outcomes are consistently worse than those of non-caregivers, with post-9/11 military caregivers consistently experiencing the worst outcomes of all.

About 20 percent of civilian and pre-9/11 military caregivers are at risk for major depression—roughly double the rate for non-caregiving adults. Post-9/11 caregivers are four times more likely than non-caregivers to be at risk.

Yoga for Caregivers. Yoga teachers and program administrators should seek to find ways to support military caregivers. These "hidden heroes" play an exceptionally critical role in caring for veterans. But, they often lack the social supports and self-care tools necessary to their own well-being. As discussed below, teaching yoga in ways that provide emotional support, encourage self-care, engage children and youth, build community, and connect to other services and supports has the potential to be enormously helpful to military and veteran family members. Finding ways to make these offerings easily available to military caregivers should be a top priority.[42]

WORKING WITH FAMILIES OF VETERANS 4: TEACH YOGA FOR EMOTIONAL SUPPORT

Teach yoga in ways that provide emotional support, and offer an easily replicable set of practices for self-care.

Generally speaking, it is most helpful to approach teaching yoga to military and veteran families as a resource for emotional support. Through the practice of yoga, interested family members can learn techniques for managing stress, reducing anxiety, alleviating depression, increasing relaxation, building resiliency, and more. General guidelines for teaching yoga in this way follow those presented above in the "Teaching and Curriculum Best Practices" section. Yoga

42 For helpful guidelines on what to say (and what not to say) to support military caregivers, see NRCHCF, 2013, and Stokes Eggleston, 2014.

teachers should keep in mind that military and veteran families may be affected by trauma, and adjust their instruction accordingly. (See also the "Best Practices for Trauma" section for a discussion of trauma-informed yoga.)

Easy Access. Yoga teachers and program administrators should consider the feasibility of offering relatively short classes (e.g., 30-60 minutes) to fit the busy schedules of parents, caregivers, and family members. Smaller class sizes are also preferable, as they provide more opportunities to learn the particular needs and concerns of students, and facilitate social connections and build community. Offering a four-week "Introduction to Yoga" class series on a regular basis provides an excellent way for family members who are unfamiliar with and/or uncertain about yoga to experiment with it in a safe, supportive setting.

Yoga teachers should keep classes simple, accessible, and welcoming. Language should be basic and descriptive, avoiding flowery language and jargon. Simple breathing exercises and easily achievable postures that can be replicated at home are best.

Yoga for Self-Care. As students start to see for themselves that yoga has positive physical and psychological effects, teachers can start to connect it to the idea of practicing self-care. Most likely, many will be unfamiliar with this concept. They may also find it difficult to imagine yoga as something that could be practiced successfully at home.

Teachers can help shift these perspectives by offering a variety of "portable" practices that are relatively easy to replicate. These could include "stop, drop, and breathe" exercises, two-minute meditations, or simple breathing patterns. Interested students can use such simple techniques as a resource for increased self-regulation, better stress management, and emotional processing. Teachers can help students see how working with themselves in this way can also empower them to navigate the inevitable challenges of family life more effectively.

Yoga for Grief and Loss. Although grief has traditionally been thought of as a psychological experience, mental health experts are beginning to realize that it involves a complex relationship between body and mind. Taught in a trauma-informed, emotionally supportive way, yoga can be an important tool to encounter sensations of grief and loss without being overwhelmed by them. This allows intense emotions, memories, and sensations to be processed in ways that support healing and increase resilience.

Yoga teachers may find it helpful to learn about the five-stage model of grief first developed by Elizabeth Kübler-Ross. Initially based on her work with terminally ill patients, this approach developed into the understanding that is normal for those who are, or have been experiencing tremendous loss to cycle between states of denial, anger, bargaining, depression, and acceptance.

For veteran families affected by illness, disability, or other service-related challenges, there is often a need to grieve the loss of a "normal" life. Taught as an emotionally supportive practice of self-care, yoga can be a resource to help families in this process. In the process, it can help them learn to embrace the possibilities of the "new normal" of life as it is today.

WORKING WITH FAMILIES OF VETERANS 5: CREATE CLASSES FOR CHILDREN AND YOUTH

Consider developing classes and/or childcare offerings to support parents, children, and youth.

Childcare is a challenge for young families, and military and veterans families are no exception. They face not only the standard issues of quality, affordability, and scheduling, but also military-specific ones such as deployments, frequent moves, and service-related injuries. Like many working parents, military parents also struggle to find childcare that can accommodate shifting work schedules, extended hours, and weekend duty. Difficult in the best of circumstances, these challenges are magnified when they must be shouldered by a single parent, or by a household that include veterans and/or other family members with disabilities.

Key ways in which yoga service providers can support military and veteran families with young children include:

- Childcare. Building a childcare option into selected adult classes makes it much easier for young parents to access the much needed stress-relieving and re-energizing qualities of yoga. Since paying for a yoga class and childcare at the same time is prohibitive for most families, it is ideal to offer childcare for free whenever possible. Teachers may be able to set up a work/trade arrangement, in which someone who is qualified to look after young children volunteers services in exchange for free classes.

  Yoga programs interested in pursuing this option should take care to: 1) follow any applicable laws and regulations; 2) set up and maintain a clean, safe, fun, and age-appropriate space; and 3) vet any individual working with young children thoroughly. Given that these are substantial demands, such an arrangement might work best in partnership with a social service agency, community center, or other organization that already provides childcare regularly.

- Parent/Child Classes. "Mommy and Me" and "Daddy and Me" yoga classes eliminate the need for childcare, at least for families with only one young child. They can also help strengthen the physical and emotional attunement between parent and child in ways that support sensory and affect regulation. To accomplish these aims, classes need to be fun, and offer bonding opportunities.

  Program administrators should be aware that teaching yoga to children is a special skill set that requires additional training. Yoga teachers working with children should understand the basic stages of child development, and how to craft classes that are developmentally appropriate for different ages. There are numerous yoga service organizations that offer such trainings. As quality will vary, it is important to research the range of options thoroughly before investing in a training program.

- Children's Yoga. Yoga classes for children offered at the same time as classes for adults offer a different solution for the childcare problem.

> Yoga also offers children a range of important benefits, such as improved strength and flexibility, neuromuscular coordination, emotional regulation, and stress relief. As noted above, teachers offering these classes should have the appropriate training. Classrooms should also be vetted as safe and appropriate for the age of children involved (e.g., remove easily breakable objects, put away props such as yoga straps that could be played with in dangerous ways).

In addition to childcare, and child/parent and children's class options, yoga service providers should consider yoga classes for youth. After-school classes are helpful for working parents with tweens and younger teens, who are too old for childcare, but too young to handle large blocks of unsupervised time safely and appropriately.

Classes for teens offer the same benefits as those for adults, and can provide a much-needed respite from the demands of school, peers, and work. By offering an experience that values internal awareness over external achievement, yoga can be helpful for teens struggling with competitive pressures, body image issues, school-based anxiety, and more. Again, however, teachers working with youth should have the additional training needed to create age-appropriate offerings.[43]

WORKING WITH FAMILIES OF VETERANS 6: UNDERSTAND THE IMPACTS OF INDIVIDUAL TRAUMA ON FAMILIES

Understand how individual veterans' experiences of trauma may affect their spouse or partner, children, and other family members, and adapt classes accordingly.

Research demonstrates that trauma has a range of impacts on individual family members, their relationships with each other, and overall family functioning (NCTSN, 2016b). If a member of a military or veteran family is suffering from

43 For a detailed discussion of teaching yoga to children and youth, see Harper and Childress, 2015.

PTSD, a spouse or partner, children, close friends, and others will be affected by it.

Everyday manifestations of post-traumatic stress that place enormous stress on family members include:

- *Re-experiencing,* or an eruption of traumatic memories typically accompanied by intense emotions such as grief, guilt, fear, or anger;
- *Avoidance and numbing,* or shying away from experiences that could trigger upsetting memories, while feeling cut off from loved ones and positive emotions; and
- *Hyper-arousal,* or being stuck in a state of nervous system overdrive, often producing anxiety, irritation, difficulty sleeping, impaired concentration, and being easily startled (Price, 2016).

Although adult intimate relationships can be a source of strength in coping with trauma, the presence of trauma always places a high degree of stress on the partnership. If a couple's coping resources are stretched too thin, partners may have problems communicating, managing emotions, and experiencing intimacy. This, in turn, increases the odds of separation, breakup, or even interpersonal violence (NCTSN, 2016b).

Any children present will be affected by the symptoms of the original trauma and the above secondary impacts. In a seminal study of children of Vietnam veterans with PTSD, Harkness (1991) found three typical patterns of response: *over-identification* (the child experiences secondary traumatization, and comes to share many of the symptoms the parent with PTSD is having); *excessive care-taking* (assuming parental roles and responsibilities to compensate for the parent's difficulties), and *emotional disassociation* (this child receives little emotional support, which results in problems at school, depression, anxiety, and relational problems later in life) (Price, 2016).

Of course, these categories do not represent every possible reaction that children may have to parents with combat-related PTSD. Nor do they highlight the successes of families who have found ways to cope with and eventually overcome the challenge of trauma. They do, however, give a sense of how PTSD might impact children in military and veteran families who are struggling with it.

Reporting Requirements. Yoga teachers should be aware that in some cases, trauma and/or other intense stressors on a family could precipitate domestic violence (DV) and/or child abuse and neglect. Instructors should be aware of any laws or regulations concerning reporting requirements in cases where abuse or DV is suspected.[44] Program administrators should develop relevant protocols and resources lists for teachers to use if needed.

Trauma-Informed Yoga for Families. Yoga teachers and program administrators should be aware of both individual and familial impacts of trauma and seek to develop programs to support those impacted by it. (See the "Best Practices for Working with Trauma" section for a more detailed discussion of these issues.) For example, depending on the community involved and resources available, teachers might want to explore how best to coordinate trauma-informed yoga offerings with child and youth program options discussed above. In some cases, partner yoga can be helpful for couples impacted by trauma seeking to strengthen emotional and physical attunement, or simply to have fun together in a healthy way.

Instructors should be aware that trauma can be a highly sensitive topic. Any discussions of it must be handled with extreme care, if at all. No individual or family issues should ever be mentioned publicly. As discussed previously, yoga teachers must remember that they are not therapists, and be careful to maintain appropriate professional boundaries.

---

44 All providers subject to DOD policy must report child maltreatment to the military installation's Family Advocacy Program (NRCHCF, 2013; 20-22).

WORKING WITH FAMILIES OF VETERANS 7: BUILD COMMUNITY

Structure classes to facilitate interpersonal connection and community building.

Military and veteran family members benefit from opportunities to develop new personal connections and a sense of community. As discussed in the "Gender Considerations" section in reference to women-only classes, one way to provide such opportunities is to structure time for informal socializing into the class schedule. Another might be to offer periodic workshops that provide structured opportunities for sharing and discussion in conjunction with a yoga class. Yoga teachers and program administrators should be creative in thinking into what might work best to build community given their particular mix of students and teachers, as well as resources and constraints.

WORKING WITH FAMILIES OF VETERANS 8: CONNECT WITH OTHER SERVICES AND SUPPORTS

Explore opportunities to collaborate with community organizations, and find ways to connect military and veteran families to local and web-based supports.

Today, there are numerous service-oriented grassroots organizations and non-profits for veterans and their families dedicated to building community, providing needed supports, and bridging the civilian-military divide. Some incorporate yoga, mindfulness, and other integrative health modalities into more traditional programming to support health and wellness. Many more are open to or interested in yoga, even if they don't offer it themselves.

Yoga teachers working with military and veterans families should learn whether such organizations exist in their local community. If so, they should explore opportunities for collaboration, such as offering a brief "Intro to Yoga" session for members and staff. Even if collaboration is not possible, knowing about such resources is important, as interested students can then be referred to them as needed.

There are also many organizational resources that can be accessed online. Program administrators and/or yoga teachers may wish to develop a handout listing the most useful resources and make it available to interested students.

CONCLUSION: Yoga for Healing, Resilience, and Well-Being

In Fall 2015, the 25 Contributors to this book convened at the Omega Institute with five leaders from the Yoga Service Council to engage in a week of intensive brainstorming. The questions and issues considered at this gathering ran broad and deep. We shared, discussed, debated, and got to know each other better, both as workers dedicated to the nascent but growing field of yoga for veterans, and simply as human beings.

The process of co-creating *Best Practices for Yoga with Veterans* wasn't always easy. It was consistently infused, however, with a sense that the task we had come together to complete was meaningful and important. Individually and collectively, we were determined to accomplish our mission of making this book a reality. Doing this right required listening to and learning from other members of our diverse group, which had been intentionally designed to encompass a wide variety of life experiences, skill sets, and sources of knowledge, insight, and expertise.

As yoga teachers and practitioners, we were aware that the quality of our process of working together was as important as the final book product itself. Our commitment to creative collaboration mirrored the YSC's working definition of "yoga service" as "the intentional sharing of yoga practices that support healing and build resilience for all regardless of circumstances, taught within a context of conscious relationship rooted in self-reflection and self-inquiry" (Childress and Cohen Harper, 2016). Boiled down to basics, this perspective sees yoga service as the process of integrating three core practices: 1) mindful yoga, 2) self-reflection, and 3) respectful relationships.

By coming together to co-create this book in this way, our 30-person team hoped to lay a foundation that would serve to strengthen, enrich, and expand the field of yoga for veterans, as well as yoga service more broadly, for years to come. This is not to suggest that we believed that our small group represented some sort of expert vanguard that others should follow. On the contrary, we remain well aware that there are many other people doing excellent, inspiring work in this field—and, we're grateful for it. We hope, however, that this book will play a significant role in expanding the network of people who share our passion for sharing top-quality yoga instruction with veterans, and that the results of this growing movement will be positive, and profound.

We believe that the yoga practices presented in *Best Practices for Yoga with Veterans* have the potential to play a pivotal role in revolutionizing how we understand and support veterans' health. With over 100 Best Practices organized into nine thematic sections, this book offers many detailed specifics regarding how best to teach and practice yoga in ways that are safe, effective, empowering, sustainable, and responsive to the particularities of the military experience. Threading through and uniting these many points is an ambitious vision of the power of yoga—particularly when aligned with complementary resources and supports—to connect each person to their innate capacity for healing, resilience, and growth.

Our faith in the potential of mindful yoga is anything but blind. Rather, it's rooted not only in our personal experience as practitioners and teachers, but also the wealth of medical, psychological, scientific, and cultural knowledge we collectively bring to bear on this subject. Nor is our shared sense of hope the product of pie-in-the-sky fantasies untested by the rigors of military service and challenging life experiences. Our team includes combat veterans, disabled veterans, frontline medical providers, VA professionals, and military and veteran family members. It also includes civilians who serve the field of yoga for veterans as doctors, nurses, therapists, teachers, volunteers, researchers, writers, and more.

We believe that *Best Practices for Yoga with Veterans* makes a critical contribution to the growing movement to share yoga with veterans in ways that will help them address injuries, manage stress, and, as needed, heal trauma. These worthy goals, however, are only the beginning. We are equally committed to offering the practice of mindful yoga as a life-long resource that helps build self-awareness and self-knowledge, decrease emotional reactivity and negative mental patterning, strengthen our ability to form positive relationships, and connect to our deeper selves in ways that nurture our overall growth and development as human beings. We hope that everyone who reads *Best Practices for Yoga with Veterans* will be inspired to explore the possibilities of yoga more deeply, and share the best of what is gained through that process with others.

EDITOR, CONTRIBUTOR, AND REVIEWER BIOS

Alexandra Arbogast is a Licensed Clinical Social Worker, Registered Yoga Teacher, and Certified Massage Therapist. In 2010, she co-created the Mind-Body Medicine Program at Walter Reed National Military Medical Center, where she currently serves as Mind-Body Medicine Program Coordinator and Senior Therapist. In this role, Alexandra teaches evidence-based mind-body skills for enhanced self-management, including mindfulness, meditation, yoga, positive psychology, and relaxation techniques. She primarily works with patients in Internal Medicine, the Warrior Clinic, and the National Intrepid Center of Excellence. Alexandra's passion for sharing this work comes from her own experience as a practitioner of meditation and yoga over the past 15 years.

Peter Banitt, M.D., practices interventional and general cardiology in Portland, Oregon. He graduated from the University of Iowa College of Medicine and received his medical and cardiology training at Beth Israel Hospital, and Brigham and Women's Hospital, Boston. He has a particular interest in the role that PTSD and acute and chronic stress have on cardiovascular diseases, and has spoken in the U.S. and internationally on these topics.

Lilly Bechtel is a Kripalu and trauma-sensitive yoga instructor and freelance journalist with eight years of experience offering yoga in alternative settings, including correctional facilities, treatment centers, and VA hospitals. Her writing has appeared in the *USA Today, Brooklyn Rail, Public Books, Faster Times, Huffington Post,* and *elephant journal,* where her series "At Attention, At Peace" explored the role of mindfulness in addressing PTSD in the military. She is currently working on a book on this topic, which will be published in Fall 2016.

Yael Calhoun, MA, MS, E-RYT is a long-time educator and author with a strong background in education and teaching yoga as a tool to address trauma, stress, depression, anxiety and compassion fatigue. She is a writer/series editor of over a dozen books, and continues to develop books, DVDs, CDs, and training manuals on yoga for trauma, autism, children, seniors, caregivers, classrooms, and cancer survivors. Yael is the co-founder and Executive Director of GreenTREE Yoga, a 501c3 nonprofit charity dedicated to bringing the benefits of yoga to people of all ages and abilities in a variety of settings, including schools, prisons, community organizations, substance abuse recovery centers, and senior centers. She has developed professional development trainings for CE credits for clinicians, psychologists, and nurses. Yael started the trauma-sensitive yoga program for PTSD, MST, and pain at the Salt Lake VA (Utah), which continues to grow. Her current project is developing a training guide for people working with refugee populations.

Beryl Bender Birch has been an avid student of yoga and the study of consciousness since 1971, and is a world-renowned yoga teacher and author. She holds degrees in English and philosophy, has traveled extensively in India, and has taught classical yoga and Vedantic and Buddhist philosophy for four decades. In 2000, she was chosen as one of seven American women named by *Yoga Journal* as "Innovators Shaping Yoga Today." In 2013, her work of co-founding and furthering the Give Back Yoga Foundation earned her the International Association of Yoga Therapists' Karma Yoga Award for "extraordinary selfless service in reducing suffering and elevating consciousness through yoga." Beryl is the director-founder of The Hard and The Soft Yoga Institute, and author of the best-selling books *Power Yoga, Beyond Power Yoga, Boomer Yoga,* and *Yoga For Warriors.*

Robin Carnes is a leading pioneer in the effort to address the urgent needs of veterans and their families with effective mind-body approaches. In 2006, Robin was the instructor for the first DOD-funded study of yoga for PTSD. From 2006-2012, Robin was the yoga and iRest® meditation instructor for an acute PTSD treatment program at Walter Reed Medical Center. Out of this work, she co-founded Warriors at Ease, which has trained over 600 yoga teachers to teach safely and effectively in military communities. In 2013, the Smithsonian Institute honored Robin for her work with the military. She has been featured in the *Washington Post, Woman's Day, Army Magazine,* and an award-winning documentary, "Escape Fire: The Fight to Rescue America's Healthcare." She has presented at numerous DOD and VA conferences on the use of complementary therapies for combat stress-related conditions, and been a frequent lecturer at the National Defense University.

Jessica-Patrice D. Coulter has been practicing yoga for over a decade. She discovered the healing, restorative power of yoga while recovering from an injury while she was recovering from an injury while she was in the U.S. Air Force. As a disabled veteran with PTSD/MST and single mother of two young sons, one of whom has autism, Jessica knows that the stillness found within the practice of yoga is the truest way for peace, both internally and externally. In addition to her 250-hour training with the Amrit Yoga Institute, she holds a certificate in pre-natal yoga from Finding Inner Peace Yoga School. She was also trained in The Veterans Yoga Project, Therapeutic Yoga for Trauma Recovery and Resiliency. Currently, she is enrolled in a M.A. program in Holistic Counseling and Expressive Arts at Salve Regina University. Jessica is also an accomplished spoken word poetry artist in the New England Area, performing as Jessica9Names or J9. In poetry, she uses her words to open minds, tell her story, and usher in healing, as with her yoga practice.

Lisa Danylchuk, EdM, LMFT, E-RYT-500, is a psychotherapist and yoga instructor passionate about integrating yoga into mental health treatment. For over 15 years, Lisa has served as a therapist and yoga teacher in prisons, schools, nonprofits and community programs across the U.S. Lisa earned her undergraduate degree at UCLA, completed her master's work and advanced studies at Harvard University, and has since presented her work to mental heath providers and yogis around the world. She is the author of the bestselling book, *Embodied Healing: Using Yoga to Recover from Trauma and Extreme Stress,* and founder of the Yoga for Trauma (Y4T) online training program. She serves on the UN Task Force for the International Society for the Study of Trauma and Dissociation (ISSTD), and on the board of Your Strength to Heal, an organization serving survivors of sexual exploitation and abuse.

Janet Durfee is an advance practice nurse who has worked for Veterans Health Administration (VHA) since 1999. Prior to that, she served in the U.S. Nurse Corps; as a RN in pediatrics, critical care, and cardiac care; and as an Adult Nurse Practitioner in primary care, women's health and hepatology. Deputy Chief Consultant for Clinical Public Health in VHA from 2008-2015, Janet currently serves as a Special Assistant to Deputy Chief, Patient Care Services in the VHA. She has both a personal and professional commitment to complementary and integrative health (CIH), and has incorporated integrated health services into her care since she began her nursing career in 1989, including Reiki, therapeutic touch, acupressure, guided imagery, and Mindfulness Based Stress Reduction. Janet has been instrumental in providing policy guidance for CIH implementation for the VHA, and a champion for expanding CIH services across this large healthcare system.

Pamela Stokes Eggleston, MS, MBA, RYT-500 is the founder and CEO of Yoga2Sleep, an organization that uses yoga and wellness services to promote "better sleep for the best life." She is a co-founder of Blue Star Families, a national nonprofit that bridges the gap between civilian and military/veteran communities and leaders. Pamela has worked for the Substance Abuse and Mental Health Services Administration, the VA, and the Department of Labor and as an advisor on Congress-supported publications centering on substance abuse, mental health, criminal justice, and military and veteran family matters. Pamela has been a caregiver for a wounded OIF veteran for over a decade.

James Fox, MA, is the founder and director of the Prison Yoga Project, an organization dedicated to establishing yoga and mindfulness programs in prisons and rehabilitation centers worldwide. Since 2002, he has been teaching yoga and mindfulness practices to prisoners at San Quentin and other California State prisons. He developed a special program for incarcerated military veterans using innovative approaches to adapting yoga for trauma healing, and to address mental health issues related to active duty. He is the author of *Yoga: A Path for*

Healing and Recovery, an instructional manual of traditional yoga practices that is provided to prisoners throughout the U.S who request it, free of charge. James offers trauma-informed, mindfulness-based teacher trainings in the U.S. and internationally for yoga instructors interested in teaching in prisons and rehabilitation facilities, and bringing yoga to disadvantaged communities. James is also the former Program Director of the Insight Prison Project, a leading restorative justice agency involved in prisoner rehabilitation.

Rolf Gates is a former social worker and U.S. Airborne Ranger who has practiced meditation for over twenty years. He is author of *Meditations from the Mat: Daily Reflections on the Path of Yoga* (2002) and *Meditations on Intention and Being: Daily Reflections on the Path of Yoga, Mindfulness, and Compassion* (2015). Rolf conducts yoga intensives, retreats and 200/500-hour yoga teacher trainings throughout the U.S., abroad, and online. He is also a co-founder of the "Yoga, Meditation and Recovery Conference," which is held regularly at the Esalen Institute and Kripalu Center for Yoga and Health. Rolf's writing has been featured in several books *(Yoga and Body Image, Find Your True North: Wanderlust, Survivors on the Yoga Mat),* and numerous magazines, including *Origins, Yoga Journal, Natural Health* and *People.*

Kate Hendricks Th**omas, PhD,** is Assistant Professor of Health Promotion at Charleston Southern University. A U.S. Marine veteran and wellness coach, Kate writes about resilience building, creating strong communities, and the science of spirituality. Her behavioral health research, published in journals like *Military Behavioral Health, Advances in Social Work,* and *Gender Forum,* has been praised as "masterful" and "constructive." She is a yoga and meditation teacher, as well as the author of *Brave, Strong, and True:* The *Modern Warrior's Battle for Balance.*

Carol Horton, PhD, is author of *Yoga PhD: Integrating the Life of the Mind and the Wisdom of the Body,* and co-editor of *21st Century Yoga: Culture, Politics, and Practice.* She serves as Board Vice-President of the Yoga Service Council, and was a co-founder of Chicago's Socially Engaged Yoga Network (SEYN). A Certified Forrest Yoga Teacher, Carol trained in trauma-informed yoga with Street Yoga and the Prison Yoga Project, and has taught in a variety of settings including a drop-in center for homeless women, locked residential foster care facility, and Chicago's Cook County Jail. An ex-political science professor, Carol holds a doctorate from the University of Chicago, is the author of *Race and the Making of American Liberalism* (Oxford University Press, 2005), and has written numerous research reports for leading foundations, nonprofits, and public agencies on issues affecting low-income children and families.

Michael Huggins, RYT, CFT, is Founder and Executive Director of Transformation Yoga, a nonprofit organization teaching yoga and mindfulness as tools for personal change in drug and alcohol rehabilitation facilities, the criminal justice system, community transitional centers, and VA hospitals. He is specially trained in applying yoga practices for addiction recovery and trauma-related issues. Mike is a registered yoga instructor, and has been practicing since 2002. He teaches a variety of asana styles including Power Vinyasa, stationary, stretch yoga, chair yoga, family yoga, yoga for the back, meditation, and many others. He is also a certified fitness trainer. Michael left a successful career in the corporate world in 2009 to focus on a variety of community-based outreach programs, and further develop his yoga practice. Since that time, Mike has dedicated himself towards demystifying yoga by breaking down the powerful and positive aspects of the practice in a direct, straightforward manner that at-risk populations can relate to. He has extensively studied yoga and meditation with highly respected teachers at Kripalu, Omega, and other organizations. Mike has been on the board of several nonprofits in the greater Philadelphia area, as well as Liberation Prison Yoga in New York City. He has a Bachelor's of Science from Villanova University and a MBA from the Wharton School at the University of Pennsylvania.

Ben King, M.A., RYT, CPT, deployed to Iraq in 2006 as a Psychological Operations Sergeant in the U.S. Army. After his service ended, Ben earned a MA in Public Anthropology from American University and devoted his thesis to an examination of the American fitness culture. Concurrently, grappling with the challenges of PTSD, Ben's search for techniques to restore his pre-war physical and mental well-being led him to mindfulness meditation and yoga. Drawing on his military and academic training, he created his own fitness regimen, Mindful Personal Training, which he has used to train almost 500 clients. He also developed an innovative web-based platform called Armor Down, designed to help military service members transition back to civilian life through the use of mindfulness-based training techniques. To accomplish this, Armor Down links online content describing or demonstrating these techniques to quick response (QR) codes, which can be reproduced on a wide variety of materials and scanned by smartphones. Also, for three consecutive years, Armor Down has organized a Mindful Memorial Day observation at Arlington National Cemetery as a means of honoring the fallen in a mindful and respectful way that helps build a bridge between the warrior and civilian communities.

Olivia Kvitne E-RYT 200, RYT 500, is Founder and Director of Yoga for First Responders. She has been a lifelong yoga practitioner, and a yoga instructor since 2003. While living in Los Angeles, Olivia taught weekly trauma-sensitive yoga classes at the Los Angeles Fire Department (LAFD) Training Center, as well as presented continuing education workshops on yoga and the neurological system for LAFD, and special workshops for high-ranking command staff of the Los Angeles Police Department (LAPD). It is at LAFD where Yoga for First Responders was first born in conjunction with Dr. Robert Scott. Olivia currently teaches yoga for Carlisle, Indianola and Norwalk Fire Departments, Des Moines Veterans Association, Iowa Army National Guard and the Des Moines Police Academy. She is a staff writer and former Assistant Editor of *LA Yoga* magazine. Olivia is a member of the International Law Enforcement Educators and Trainers Association (ILEETA).

Patricia Lillis-Hearne, MD, MPH, E-RYT spent 32 years in the Army Medical department as an oncologist, ending her career having served both as a medical Commander in Iraq and working for the Army Surgeon General. A Kripalu-certified yoga instructor, she is also well versed in Complementary Medicine. Her combat experience in Operation Iraqi Freedom, as well as the care of wounded veterans led her to co-found the nonprofit Warriors at Ease, and serve as its first President. This organization has taught over 600 yoga and meditation teachers in at least seven different countries to work with veterans with PTSD, traumatic brain injuries and other war wounds. Pat's current focus is on the healing process within the individual, and teaching and consulting on program development in the U.S. and internationally.

Suzanne Manafort studied extensively with Beryl Bender Birch at The Hard and The Soft Yoga Institute, and with Patty Townsend in the Embodyoga® Teacher Training programs at Yoga Center Amherst. She is now on faculty as a teacher trainer at both schools, as well as Director of the Newington Yoga Center teacher trainings. Suzanne is co-author of the *Mindful Yoga* The*rapy for Veterans,* and producer of two CDs designed for veterans with PTSD, *Yoga Nidra* and *Breathe In Breathe Out.* Suzanne serves on the Board of the Give Back Yoga Foundation, and was designated a Wells Fargo Second Half Champion in 2009 for her work with veterans.

Annie Okerlin is founder of Yogani Studios and the Exalted Warrior Foundation, began practicing yoga in 1996. Intent on deepening her practice, Annie attended Bikram Yoga Training in 1999 and within three weeks she knew teaching yoga was her life's passion. Yogani Studios opened in 1999 as a small, one-room studio. Since that time, Annie's energy and compassion have led her to expand Yogani into a thriving community for yogis and yoga teachers in Tampa. In 2005, Annie founded the Exalted Warrior Foundation and began a new path of teaching adaptive yoga to traumatically wounded veterans. Through EWF, Annie teaches yoga to wounded populations throughout military and veterans hospitals. Annie and EWF support nationwide programs assisting the re-integration of the wounded back into civilian life. As a member of the faculty at Warriors at Ease (WAE), she teaches the adaptive training for the "Teaching Yoga in a Military Setting" and mentors teachers through their certification process.

Susan Pease Banitt, LCSW, RYT, authored the award-winning book Th*e Trauma Tool Kit: Healing PTSD From the Inside Out* (2012). She recently celebrated her 40th anniversary in mental health work, and her 30th anniversary of yogic studies and practices. Susan has a trauma-focused private practice in Portland, Oregon. She has spoken and conducted over 50 trainings on the yoga-based healing of PTSD and traumatic stress, both nationally and internationally. Susan served as co-chair of Street Yoga, Treasurer for the National Association of Social Workers

(Oregon chapter), and on the first-ever Complementary Therapies Committee Beth Israel Hospital, Boston, in 1991. Susan is a Kripalu-trained yoga instructor and studied Vedanta with Babaji Bob Kindler of SRV Associates.

Sarah Plummer Taylor, MSW, RYT-500, Certified Health Coach, and author, works in the field of resilience-building, holistic health coaching, and yoga. Her current research focuses on reintegration for veterans and holistic wellness, and she is involved with numerous collaborative research projects in these areas. Sarah's interest in veterans' reintegration is informed by personal experience: She is a former Marine Corps Intelligence Officer who spent more than six years on active duty. Sarah currently serves veterans, executives, and entrepreneurs with group and one-on-one holistic health coaching, workshops, and retreats. She is also the co-owner of JRWI Wellness, which provides unique, somatic-based stress management workshops both domestically and internationally. Sarah is the author of *Just Roll With It: 7 Battle Tested Truths for Creating a Resilient Life,* as well as the *Just Roll With It Wellness Journal.*

Audrey Schoomaker, RN, BSN, E-RYT is an Army Nurse veteran, a yoga instructor, and passionate advocate for the power of the mind to heal the body. She conducted a research study on therapeutic yoga for chronic back pain at Walter Reed, and is currently working as an Integrative Health Specialist at the Uniformed Services University creating integrative health products for the Human Performance Resource Center. She is married to Lt. General (Ret.) Eric Schoomaker, former Surgeon General of the Army, who championed the use of integrative approaches for pain management in the military.

Ann Richardson Stevens is the owner/director of Studio Bamboo Institute of Yoga, Virginia Beach, where she teaches a variety of classes emphasizing technique and alignment, intensives, and teacher trainings at the 200- and 500-hour levels. For over five years, Ann has provided classes in Adaptive Yoga to veterans, active duty men and women returning from combat, and the injured or ill, including those grappling with PTSD and TBI. Ann works with all types of disabilities including children and adults, and has developed this Adaptive Yoga Program from her experience working with these populations. She instructs workshops and teacher trainings across the country. Ann is honored to sit on the Board of the Give Back Yoga Foundation.

Kathryn Thomas, E-RYT, founded Yoga 4 Change after being medically retired from the U.S. Navy, where she served as a helicopter pilot. Having been introduced to yoga as a child by her mother, she had always thought it was strictly a physical practice. During her final months in the Navy, she began studying to become a yoga teacher through the Yoga School of Kailua. During this training, she was exposed to teaching inside the correctional facilities on the island of Oahu, and found her purpose: bringing the practice of yoga to all types of people experiencing trauma. When her husband was transferred to Jacksonville, Florida, she witnessed the need for mental, emotional, and physical healing in her new community. From this, the mission statement for a new nonprofit was created to include underserved populations in Northeast Florida: veterans, incarcerated men and woman, vulnerable youth, and those suffering from substance abuse. Kathryn is a 200 E-RYT/500 RYT, as well as a Certified Baptiste Teacher. She resides in Jacksonville with her husband and two Labrador retrievers.

Ned R. Timbel is a 62-year old retired geologist with many years of yoga background. After retirement, he and his wife founded Comeback Yoga to bring trauma-informed yoga to veterans. They teach primarily in VA facilities in Denver, CO.

Duilia "Dui" M. Turner, MBA, MA, RYT-500, is the creative director of Yoga Pollen and founder of Integrative World, a community promoting balanced lifestyles. Dui is also a military officer with 19 years of active duty service, including two deployments. She is part of the faculty for Mindful Yoga Therapy, serves on the Board of Advisors for Warrior One, and is a volunteer project coordinator for the Indra Devi Foundation. Most recently, she collaborated with the Give Back Yoga Foundation and Connected Warriors to create the "Yoga Readiness Initiative," which provides free yoga kits for members of the military. She has taught traditional and adaptive yoga at the Pentagon, various Air Force Wounded Warrior Camps, and the U.S. Southern Command. Currently, Dui lives in Florida, where she continues to share her passion for service, wellness, and quality of life.

Judy Weaver is the Director of Yoga South's Teacher Training Program in Boca Raton, Florida and is the primary founder and Director of Education for Connected Warriors. Judy is widely recognized for her expertise and knowledge of yoga and other mind/body disciplines, regularly conducting 200- and 500-hour certified yoga teacher trainings, facilitating workshops, and lecturing on the college and university level. Judy conducts Trauma Conscious Yoga trainings, developing curriculum based on the latest scientific and psychological research available for yoga as a healing modality for traumatic stress. Judy was appointed to Yoga Alliance's Schools and Studios advisory board in 2012.

Alison Whitehead is a RYT-500 with a Master's in Public Health from Columbia University, Mailman School of Public Health. She began working for the Women's Health Services office at the VA Central Office in 2010 as a Presidential Management Fellow, and was inspired to become a yoga teacher by colleagues who were teaching yoga to veterans at VA Medical Centers. Alison has taught yoga for athletes, indoor cycling, and high intensity interval classes in the community, and co-developed a yoga for PTSD program at the Manhattan VA Medical Center in 2014. Alison is currently a Program Manager for the Integrative Health Coordinating Center, VHA Office of Patient Centered Care and Cultural Transformation.

GLOSSARY/USEFUL TERMINOLOGY

AKA: Above the knee amputation

Base: Air Force or Navy installation

BKA: Below the knee amputation

Camp: Marine Corps installation

CO: Commanding Officer, often basically the service member's "boss."

CONUS/OCONUS: Continental United States, Outside the Continental United States.

DADT: "Don't Ask, Don't Tell," a policy holding that gays and lesbians could remain in the military as long as they did not openly declare their sexual orientation which was in effect during 1993-2011.

EAS: End of Active Service

ETS: Estimated Termination of Service, the date a service member is expected to leave service. It is established at the beginning of an enlistment or entrance on active duty. The term 'estimated' is used because it could change during the service time, for example due to a medical extension or discharge, or due to voluntary extension in the form of another tour.

Garrison: a military post; especially, a permanent military installation.

GI Bill: Any of several VA education benefit programs earned by members of Active Duty, Selected Reserve and National Guard Armed Forces and their families.

HIPAA: Health Insurance Portability and Accountability Act

Infection Control: Policies and procedures used to help prevent the spread of infection; these are mandated in every hospital and clinic, civilian or military.

JAG: Judge Advocate General; the legal branch of each of the services. Also a term used for a lawyer, as in "going to see the JAG."

LGBTQ: Lesbian Gay Bisexual Transgender Queer

MJIA: Military Justice Improvement Act

MP: Military Police (Air Force is SF, Security Forces)

MST: Military Sexual Trauma

OIF: Operation Iraqi Freedom

OEF: Operation Enduring Freedom

OND: Operation New Dawn

OpTempo: Operational Tempo or Operations Tempo, indicating the pace of workflow and workload.

Orthostatic hypotension (also called postural hypotension): A form of low blood pressure that happens when moving from sitting or lying down to standing up, which can lead to lightheadedness or even fainting. Symptoms may be more problematic with hot temperatures, dehydration or certain prescription medications.

OT: Occupational therapy

PCS: Permanent change of station (relocating)

PDA: Post Deployment Assessment

PDHA: Post Deployment Health Assessment

PDHRA: Post Deployment Health Re-Assessment

POC: Point of Contact (designated staff person in the VA)

Post: Army installation

Prosthesis: Adaptive artificial device that replaces a missing body part, such as an artificial leg.

PCS: Permanent Change of Station; the term used when a service member is transferred to another location.

PRRC: Psychosocial Rehabilitation and Reintegration Center

PFT: Physical Fitness Test; mandatory testing every 6 months to assess physical fitness. The testing standards are different for each of the services, but all are scored on a point system that for enlisted personnel typically impacts the point system used for promotion. There are some variations built into the tests to accommodate injuries (termed being on a medical "Profile".) Failure on a PT test is serious and if not rectified before the annual evaluation severely impacts a service member's career.

PT: Physical therapy

PT: Physical Training (e.g., working out)

PTS/PTSD: Post Traumatic Stress Disorder

SAV Act: The Clay Hunt Suicide Prevention Act for American Veterans

TBI/mTBI: Traumatic Brain Injury, mild Traumatic Brain Injury.

TDY/TAD: Temporary Duty/Temporary Assigned Duty

UA: Unauthorized Absence (AWOL for Marine Corps and Navy)

UCMJ: Uniformed Code of Military Justice (the foundation of military law)

VA: Department of Veterans Affairs

VHA: Veterans Health Administration

XO: Executive Officer

REFERENCES

afterdeployment.org. (2015). Just the facts: Military sexual trauma. Retrieved August 25, 2016 from http://afterdeployment.dcoe.mil/sites/default/files/pdfs/client-handouts/mst-sexual-assault-harassment.pdf

Banks, S. (2014, November 10). A female navy veteran recalls the harassment and humiliation. *Los Angeles Times*. Retrieved March 30, 2016 from http://www.latimes.com/local/california/la-me-1111-banks-female-veterans-20141111-column.html

Bateman, G. W. (2004). Military culture: United States. glbtq, inc.

Blue Star Families/Vulcan Productions. (2013). Everyone serves: A handbook for family and friends of service members during pre-deployment, deployment, and reintegration. Retrieved April 17, 2016 from http://www.everyoneservesbook.com/downloads/EveryoneServes.pdf

Brenner, L. A., and Barnes, S. M. (2012). Facilitating treatment engagement during high-risk transition periods: A potential suicide prevention strategy. *American Journal of Public Health | Supplement, 102*(S1).

Castaneda, L. W. et al. (2008). Deployment experiences of Guard and Reserve families: Implications for support and retention. Santa Monica, CA: RAND Corp. Retrieved April 15, 2016 from http://www.rand.org/content/dam/rand/pubs/monographs/2008/RAND_MG645.pdf

Childress, T., and Cohen Harper, J. (Feb. 2016). What is yoga service? A working definition. *Yoga Service Community Resource Paper*. Retrieved May 27, 2016 from https://yogaservicecouncil.org/wp-content/uploads/2016/03/YSC_CRP-WhatIsYogaService.pdf

Clever, M., and Segal, D. R. (2013). The demographics of military children and families. The *Future of Children, Fall* 23(2).

Cochran, B. N. et al. (2013). Mental health characteristics of sexual minority veterans. *Journal of Homosexuality, 60*, 419–435.

Coeytaux, R. R. et al. (2014, August). Evidence map of yoga for high-impact conditions affecting veterans. Department of Veterans Affairs, Health Services Research and Development Service. Washington, DC. Retrieved July 14, 2016 from http://www.hsrd.research.va.gov/publications/esp/yoga-EXEC.pdf

Daly, M. (2014, November 10). VA announces 'MyVA' plan, largest reorganization in department's history. *PBS Newshour*. Retrieved April 22, 2016 from http://www.pbs.org/newshour/rundown/va-announces-myva-plan-largest-reorganization-departments-history/

Danylchuk, L. (2015). *Embodied healing: Using yoga to recover from trauma and extreme stress.* Washington, DC: Difference Press.

Dunivin, K. O. (1997, February). Military culture: A paradigm shift? Air War College Maxwell Paper No. 10. Maxwell AFB, AL. Retrieved March 29, 2016 from http://www.au.af.mil/au/awc/awcgate/maxwell/mp10.pdf

Ehrenfreund, M. (2015, September 2). The problem with becoming a yoga instructor. *Washington Post.* Retrieved March 1, 2016 from https://www.washingtonpost.com/news/wonk/wp/2015/09/02/the-problem-with-becoming-a-yoga-instructor/

Emerson, D., and Hopper, E. (2011). *Overcoming trauma through yoga: Reclaiming your body.* Berkeley, CA: North Atlantic Books.

Fallows, J. (2015, February). The tragedy of the American military. The *Atlantic.* Retrieved March 1, 2016 from http://www.theatlantic.com/magazine/archive/2015/01/the-tragedy-of-the-american-military/383516/

Federal Bureau of Prisons (FBP). (n.d.) Inmate gender. FBP web resource. Retrieved April 20, 2015 from https://www.bop.gov/about/statistics/statistics_inmate_gender.jsp

Feuerstein, G. (2001). The *yoga tradition: Its history, literature, philosophy and practice* (3rd ed.). Chino Valley, AZ: Hohm Press.

Gallagher, R. M. (2016). Chronification of pain and the science of pain management. *Forum,* Spring. Washington, DC: U.S. Department of Veterans Affairs. Retrieved July 16, 2016 from http://www.hsrd.research.va.gov/publications/internal/forum-spring2016.pdf

Halvorson, A. (2010). Understanding the military: The institution, the culture, and the people: Information for behavioral healthcare specialists working with veterans and service members. Partners for Recovery/SAMHSA. Retrieved February 26, 2015 from http://www.samhsa.gov/sites/default/files/military_white_paper_final.pdf

Harper, J. C., and Childress, T. (2015). *Best practices for yoga in schools.* NY: YSC/Omega Books.

Hendricks Thomas, K. (2015). *Brave, strong, true:* The *modern warrior's battle for balance.* Innovo Publishing.

Hendricks Thomas, K., and Plummer Taylor, S. (2015). Bulletproofing the psyche: Mindfulness interventions in the training environment to improve resilience in the military and veteran communities. *Advances in Social Work 16*(2), 312–322.

Horton, C. (2016). Yoga is not dodgeball: Mind-body integration and progressive education. In Beth Berila, Melanie Klein, and Chelsea Jackson (Eds.), *Yoga, the body,and embodied social change: An intersectional feminist analysis.* NY: Lexington Books.

Hoyt, T., Klosterman Rielage, J., and Williams, L. F. (2011). Military Sexual Trauma in men: A review of reported rates. *Journal of Trauma and Dissociation, 12,* 244–260.

Lennard, N. (2012, October 15). U.S. has more prisoners, prisons than any other country. *Salon.* Retrieved April 22, 2016 from http://www.salon.com/2012/10/15/us_has_more_prisoners_prisons_than_any_other_country/

Mallinson, J., and Singleton, M. (2016). *Roots of yoga: A sourcebook from the Indian traditions.* NY: Penguin Classics, forthcoming.

Malmin, M. M. (2013). Warrior culture, spirituality, and prayer. *Journal of Religion and Health* (52)3, 740–758.

Manafort, S., and Gilmartin, R. (2013). *Mindful Yoga Therapy for Veterans Recovering from Trauma.* Boulder, CO: Give Back Yoga Foundation.

Medlin, S. R. (2014). Demographic profile: Yoga. Scribd.com typescript. Retrieved April 20, 2016 from https://www.scribd.com/doc/203990542/Demographic-Profile-Yoga

Miller, K., and Cray, A. (2013, September 20). The battles that remain: Military service and LGBT equality. *Center for American Progress.*

National Center for Veterans Analysis and Statistics (NCVAS). (2011). *America's women veterans: Military service history and VA benefit utilization statistics.* Washington, DC: U.S. Department of Veterans Affairs. Retrieved March 30, 2016 from http://www.va.gov/vetdata/docs/specialreports/final_womens_report_3_2_12_v_7.pdf

National Child Traumatic Stress Network (NCTSN). (2016). Complex trauma. Retrieved April 13, 2016 (a) from http://www.nctsn.org/trauma-types/complex-trauma

National Child Traumatic Stress Network (NCTSN). (2016). Families and trauma. Retrieved April 20, 2016 (b) from http://www.nctsn.org/resources/topics/families-and-trauma

National Resource Center for Healthy Children and Families (NRCHCF). (2013). U.S. Department of Health and Human Services, Administration for Children and Families. A support and resource guide for working with military families. Retrieved April 21, 2016 from http://www.acf.hhs.gov/sites/default/files/ofa/msp.pdf

Noonan, M. E., and Mumola, C. J. (2007, May). Veterans in state and federal prison 2004. *Bureau of Justice Statistics Special Report* (Washington, DC: U.S. Department of Justice). Retrieved April 25, 2016 from http://www.bjs.gov/content/pub/pdf/vsfp04.pdf

Pence, P. G. (2013-14, Winter). Bringing yoga to the veterans administration health care system: Wisdom from the journey. *Journal of Yoga Service.* Retrieved March 1, 2016 from https://www.iayt.org/resource/.../journalyogaservice_pence_bri.pdf

Petersen, H. (2015, August 25). I served in the active military. Yes, I'm one! Veterans Health Administration, U.S. Dept. of Veterans Affairs. Retrieved March 30, 2016 from http://www.va.gov/health/newsfeatures/2015/august/I-Served-Active-Military-Yes-Im-One.asp

Philipps, D. (2015, September 6). Ousted as gay, aging veterans are battling again for honorable discharges. *New York Times.* Retrieved February 26, 2015 from http://www.nytimes.com/2015/09/07/us/gay-veterans-push-for-honorable-discharges-they-were-denied.html

Plummer Taylor, S. (2015). *Just roll with it: 7 Battle tested truths for building a resilient life.* (3rd ed.). Collierville, TN: Innovo Publishing.

Price, J. L. (2016). Children of veterans and adults with PTSD. American Academy of Experts in Traumatic Stress. Retrieved April 21, 2016 from http://www.aaets.org/article188.htm

Ramchand, R, Tanielian, T., and Adamson, D. M. (2014). Hidden heroes: America's military caregivers serve in the shadow of war — and of the wounded. *RAND Review,* Spring. Retrieved April 18, 2016 from http://www.rand.org/pubs/periodicals/rand-review/issues/2014/spring/caregivers.html

Rosenberg, M. (2016, June 30). Transgender people will be allowed to serve openly in military. *New York Times.* Retrieved August 25, 2016 from http://www.nytimes.com/2016/07/01/us/transgender-military.html

Schmalzl, L. and Kerr, C. E. (2016). Neural mechanisms underlying movement-based embodied contemplative practices. *Frontiers in Human Neuroscience* (e-book). Retrieved July 14, 1016 from http://journal.frontiersin.org/researchtopic/1899/neural-mechanisms-underlying-movement-based-embodied-contemplative-practices

Schmalzl, L., Powers, C., and Henje Blom, E. (2015). Neurophysiological and neurocognitive mechanisms underlying the effects of yoga-based practices: Towards a comprehensive theoretical framework. *Frontiers in Human Neuroscience* 235. Retrieved March 28, 2015 from http://journal.frontiersin.org/article/10.3389/fnhum.2015.00235/full

Segal, M. W. (1986). The military and the family as greedy institutions. *Armed Forces and Society, (13)*1, 9–38. doi: 10.1177/0095327X8601300101

Shulkin, D. J. (2016). Beyond the VA crisis: Becoming a high-performance network. *New England Journal of Medicine* 374, 1003-1005. Retrieved May 25, 2016 from http://www.nejm.org/doi/full/10.1056/NEJMp1600307

Singleton, M. (2010). *Yoga body:* The *origins of modern posture practice.* NY: Oxford University Press.

Szymendera, Scott D. "Who Is a "Veteran"? Basic Eligibility for Veterans' Benefits," *Congressional Research Service* (Aug. 19, 2015), accessed May 5, 2016, https://www.fas.org/sgp/crs/misc/R42324.pdf

Segal, Mady Wechsler. "The Military and the Family as Greedy Institutions," *Armed Forces and Society* 13, no. 1 (1986), 9–38, doi: 10.1177/0095327X8601300101

Southwell, K. H., and MacDermid Wadsworth, S. M. (2016, January). The many faces of military families: Unique features of the lives of female service members. *Military Medicine (181)*1. 70–79.

Stander, V. A., and Thomsen, C. J. (2016, January). Sexual harassment and assault in the U.S. Military: A review of policy and research trends. *Military Medicine, (181),* 20–27.

Stokes Eggleston, P. (2014). Why military and veteran families matter. Sedona Yoga Festival blog. Retrieved April 18, 2016 from http://sedonayogafestival.com/syf2014-presenters/why-military-and-veteran-families-matter-by-2014syf-presenter-pamela-stokes-eggleston/

Szymendera, S. D. (2015, August 19). Who is a "veteran"? Basic eligibility for veterans' benefits. *Congressional Research Service*. Retrieved May 5, 2016 from https://www.fas.org/sgp/crs/misc/R42324.pdf

Tedeschi, R. G., and Calhoun, L. G. (2004). Posttraumatic growth: Conceptual foundations and empirical evidence. *Psychological Inquiry, 15*(1), 1–18.

Tilghman, A. (2015, December 3). All combat jobs open to women in the military. *Military Times*. Retrieved March 30, 2016 from http://www.militarytimes.com/story/military/pentagon/2015/12/03/carter-telling-military-open-all-combat-jobs-women/76720656/

U.S. Census Bureau. (rev. 2015, July). A snapshot of our nation's veterans. Retrieved March 30, 2015 from https://www.census.gov/library/infographics/veterans.html

U.S. Dept. of Veteran's Affairs (VA). (2015, July 30). MyVA Integrated Plan. Retrieved April 25, 2016 from http://www.va.gov/opa/myva/docs/myva_integrated_plan.pdf

U.S. Dept. of Veteran's Affairs (VA). (2011, September). 2011 Complementary and Integrative Medicine. Retrieved July 18, 2016 from http://www.research.va.gov/research_topics/2011cam_finalreport.pdf

U.S. Dept. of Veteran's Affairs (VA). (2015, January 26). VA announces single regional framework under MyVA initiative. Retrieved April 25, 2016 from http://www.blogs.va.gov/VAntage/16786/va-announces-single-regional-framework-under-myva-initiative/

van der Kolk, B. (2014). The *body keeps the score: Brain, mind, and body in the healing of trauma*. NY: Viking.

Warren, J. (2008). One in 100: Behind bars in America 2008. Washington, DC: Pew Charitable Trusts. Retrieved April 26, 2016 from http://www.pewtrusts.org/~/media/legacy/uploadedfiles/wwwpewtrustsorg/reports/sentencing_and_corrections/onein100pdf.pdf

Wood, David. (2014, March). Moral injury (3-part series). The *Huffington Post*. Retrieved Feb. 26, 2016 from http://projects.huffingtonpost.com/projects/moral-injury

Yoga Alliance. (n.d.). Yoga teacher designations. Retrieved March 10, 2016 from https://www.yogaalliance.org/Credentialing/Credentials_for_Teachers/Yoga_Teacher_Designations

Zarembo, A. (2015, June 8). Suicide rate of female military veterans is called "staggering." *Los Angeles Times*. Retrieved March 17, 2016 from http://www.latimes.com/nation/la-na-female-veteran-suicide-20150608-story.html